CONTENTS

INTRODUCTION............5
Getting to know the
  Black Sea resorts 8
The best of the Black Sea
  resorts 10
Symbols key 12

RESORTS.................................13
Balchik..14
Albena...18
Golden Sands 23
St Constantine and Elena...........29
Varna...33
Sunny Beach...................................39
Nessebar 45
Pomorie..51
Sozopol...53
Primorsko...58
Ahtopol...60

EXCURSIONS........................63
Excursions in the north 65
  Srebarna Nature Reserve 65
  Kaliakra Nature Reserve............66
  Dobrich 74
Excursions in the south..............79
  Bourgas 79
  Bourgas Lakes...............................
  Strandzha (Strandja)
    National Park................

LIFESTYLE...............................91
Food & drink...................................92
Menu decoder 96
Shopping 98
Children 102
Sports & activities 104
Festivals & events.......................106

PRACTICAL INFORMATION...109
Accommodation 110
Preparing to go............................112
During your stay..........................115

INDEX 125

MAPS
Black Sea resorts 6
Golden Sands...................................22
Varna..32
Sunny Beach 40
Nessebar 46
Sozopol..54
Bourgas..78

WHAT'S IN YOUR GUIDEBOOK?

Independent authors Impartial up-to-date information from our travel experts who meticulously source local knowledge.

Experience Thomas Cook's 165 years in the travel industry and guidebook publishing enriches every word with expertise you can trust.

Travel know-how Thomas Cook has thousands of staff working around the globe, all living and breathing travel.

Editors Travel-publishing professionals, pulling everything together to craft a perfect blend of words, pictures, maps and design.

You, the traveller We deliver a practical, no-nonsense approach to information, geared to how you really use it.

▶ *The Cathedral of the Assumption in Varna*

INTRODUCTION
Getting to know the Black Sea resorts

Black Sea

Bulgaria

Romania
Italy   Bulgaria
Greece

Ahtopol

Tsarevo

Nessebar   Primorsko

Sunny Beach

Pomorie   Sozopol

Bourgas
BOURGAS

A4

Aitos

Sredets

Karnobat

Strandzha National Park

TURKEY

Yambol

**Bulgaria:
Black Sea resorts**

0   30 km
0   20 miles

Getting to know the Black Sea resorts

The Black Sea is three hours or less from most of Europe's capitals, and its golden sands, warm shallow waters, hot summer sunshine and great-value prices have made it a favourite of holidaymakers since the late 1970s. Bulgaria is a Balkan nation, and offering fine hospitality is second nature here, alongside a love of street commerce, fine wine and simple but tasty food.

⬥ *Flying high over Sunny Beach*

To all intents and purposes Bulgaria's Black Sea coast is made up of two enormous bays. Two distinct groups of resorts sit in each, satellites almost of two major cities on the coast: Varna in the north, and Bourgas in the south. In between, fishing villages 2,000 years old provide quiet respite from the party atmosphere of the larger resorts.

Heading northwards from Varna, the bay arcs round, via the Golden Sands resort, to Cape Kaliakra. The contrast perfectly sums up the variety of the coast. Leave Golden Sands – a purpose-built temple to pleasure, chock-full of hotels, restaurants offering full English breakfasts and beach activities – and after an hour's drive, you'll find yourself on a remote, windy cliff top that seems to have changed little from the Middle Ages, from where you can occasionally spot dolphins in the sea far below.

When large numbers of foreign visitors first began arriving on Bulgaria's beaches at the end of the 1970s, many could have been forgiven for thinking that life under communism wasn't all that bad. Warm waters lapping the golden sands of the Black Sea shore, hot sunny weather, friendly locals and gallons of cheap, excellent wine made holidays here memorable. Bulgaria's communists, though harshly authoritarian, never managed to quell the Balkan instinct for trade and commerce, hospitality and making money. That is one reason that Bulgaria never suffered the shortages and deprivations that hit neighbouring Romania.

When the changes of 1989 swept the communists away, Bulgaria was already established as a favourite summer holiday destination. It has since become a popular holiday spot for Britons, whose rush to snap up local property has created a sizeable expat contingent.

Bulgaria has embraced this foreign invasion and the tourism industry has responded with enthusiasm to visitors' wishes and needs. While peaceful villages and quiet beaches await those who want to get away from it all, the larger resorts provide every home comfort, from British tea to tabloid newspapers. Local sensitivities have adapted to Western ways and every foreign taste – be it topless sunbathing or a fry-up – is catered for.

THE BEST OF THE BLACK SEA RESORTS

Though it may not be the first place you think of for holidays by the sea, Bulgaria's Black Sea coast ticks all the right boxes. Whether you want watersports or nightlife, picturesque seaside villages, beautiful wildernesses or tradition and culture, you'll find it here.

TOP 10 ATTRACTIONS

- **Seafood at Nessebar** It may look as if there are more seafood restaurants at Nessebar than people to fill them, but prices are reasonable and quality is high. Everything will be fresh from the sea that day (see page 49).

- **Pomorie** Quieter and more secluded than Nessebar, Pomorie is the centre of Bulgaria's mud treatment industry; most of the village's hotels offer treatments (see page 51).

- **Varna's cathedral** Majestic in every way from its monolithic size to its golden decoration, Varna's cathedral of 1886 is guaranteed to take your breath away (see page 35).

- **Beach at Golden Sands** Golden Sands – a literal translation of the Bulgarian name Zlatni Pyusnati – is not the invention of an optimistic marketing man's imagination: the sand here really is as gold as you could possibly wish for (see page 23).

- **Queen Marie's palace at Balchik** Romania's Queen Marie (who was English and a granddaughter of Queen Victoria) built a superb, oriental-style palace here, surrounded by the beautiful Botanic Gardens (see pages 15–16).

- **Storks on the Bourgas Lakes** Birdwatchers are in for a treat in Bulgaria: a wonderful array of birds, such as storks and pelicans, can be found in the marshes and lakes of Bourgas, a unique and carefully protected ecosystem (see page 86).

- **Cliffs at Kaliakra Nature Reserve** Another birdwatcher's paradise, this time with plenty for non-twitchers too. The shoreline here is steep, beautiful, remote and heavily protected (see page 66).

- **Concerts at Sozopol's amphitheatre** Re-create the atmosphere of Roman Apollonia at the Apollonia Arts Festival, held every September in the peninsula's amphitheatre. The sea provides the perfect dramatic backdrop (see page 55).

- **Nightlife** Golden Sands and Sunny Beach are the Black Sea's leading nightlife destinations. Clubbers will have no trouble finding places in which to dance until dawn (see pages 28 and 43–4).

- **Watersports at Albena** Powered watersports are cheap in Bulgaria, and Albena is the place for every kind of water-based fun (see page 20).

◆ *The Botanic Gardens at beautiful Balchik*

SYMBOLS KEY

The following symbols are used throughout this book:

⊚ address ☎ telephone ☎ fax ⓦ website address ⓔ email
🕐 opening times ⓝ public transport connections ⓘ important

The following symbols are used on the maps:

𝒊	information office	⭕	city
✉	post office	⭕	large town
🛍	shopping	○	small town
✈	airport	◼	point of interest
➕	hospital	═	motorway
🛡	police station	—	main road
🚌	bus station	—	minor road
🚆	railway station	—	railway
✝	church		
➊	numbers denote featured cafés, restaurants & evening venues		

RESTAURANT CATEGORIES
The symbol after the name of each restaurant listed in this guide
indicates the price of a typical three-course meal without drinks
for one person:
£ under L15   ££ L15–L30   £££ over L30

▶ *The scenic coastline at Nessebar*

RESORTS
Places under the sun

Balchik

Queen Marie of Romania adored Balchik. On more than one occasion she described it as her favourite place in Romania: the fact that it was once in Romania at all betrays the troubled history of the region. Returned to Bulgaria in 1940 (it had been annexed in 1913 by Romania after the Second Balkan War), the town is most famous as the site of the **Royal Palace**, built by Queen Marie in the 1920s and 1930s, which sits in some splendid **Botanic Gardens**.

Today, Balchik is at peace. Rustic villas with terracotta roofs nestle among the trees on the hillside overlooking the sea, in a scene that could be straight from an early 20th-century painting. The town's attractions – including a certain authenticity and unspoiled charm – have not been lost on visitors, but the influx of tourists has not overwhelmed Balchik. Narrow cobbled streets wind sharply upwards – and are just as likely to take you to an isolated field as a smart restaurant. Take a relaxing walk and you will notice something missing from the typical seaside resort: noise. The hustle and bustle of holidaymakers is replaced by the sound of the sea breeze or an occasional bird.

This is not to say that hoteliers and restaurateurs have neglected Balchik. On the contrary, the town has some of the finest hotels in the area, almost all of which are minutes from the sea, if not on the seafront itself, and the relative quietness of the resort keeps prices reasonable. The rural atmosphere might not suggest it, but Balchik has its fair share of culture too. This makes it a good choice for anyone who wants to spend a few days getting away from the crowds without breaking the bank.

BEACHES

Balchik's beach is not generally as crowded as those of the more touristy resorts on the Black Sea coast, and you won't have to fight for a spot on the sand. The zoom of high-octane watersports is replaced by the distant chug of fishing boats as they pootle back and forth. From the beach, you'll also have a view of the fishermen trying out their luck on the small jetties. Indeed, this place is more about fishing than sun-worshipping, and attracts those after a bit of privacy and calm.

THINGS TO SEE & DO

Botaniceski Gradina (Botanic Gardens)

Charming though Queen Marie's palace is (see below), it is almost outshone by the Botanic Gardens that surround it. In contrast to the ruggedness of the town, here nature is neat and well tended, with flowerbed after flowerbed alive with red, yellow, white and purple blooms. Gentle streams babble along, cottages are hidden among the trees, while a gushing waterfall provides a brief glimpse of nature untamed.

The gardens total 6.5 hectares (16 acres), and it is quite easy to get lost along the leaf-covered walkways or down the steps carved out of the hillside. It's equally easy to while away several hours just pottering around and discovering new sections. Benches are tucked away in hedges, which afford you some privacy as you sit and take in the scenery while recovering from the walking and climbing.

ⓐ 3 km (2 miles) west of town on the E87 ⓣ 0579 76854 ⓦ www.dvoreca.com ⓔ office@dvoreca.com ⓛ 08.00–20.00 daily (May–mid-Oct); 08.30–18.30 daily (mid-Oct–Apr) ⓘ Admission charge, which includes the Royal Palace

Dvoreca (Royal Palace)

By far Balchik's biggest crowd-puller is Queen Marie's palace. The Kent-born aristocrat was a descendant of Queen Victoria and the palace betrays a typical English gentility. Unlike some of the garish communist-era constructions that sprang up elsewhere in the region, the palace is understated, bearing more resemblance to a country villa than a royal seat, despite the minaret rising up from the roof that gives a nod to Islamic culture. Queen Marie would certainly have enjoyed the view from her residence, which looks straight out to sea and the cliffs further along the strip of coast.

🅐 3 km (2 miles) west of town on the E87 🕕 0579 76854
🅦 www.dvoreca.com 🅔 office@dvoreca.com 🕒 08.00–20.00 daily
(May–mid-Oct); 08.30–18.30 daily (mid-Oct–Apr) 🅘 Admission charge,
which includes entrance to the Botanical Gardens

Etnografski Muzei (Ethnographic Museum)

Opposite the Municipal Historical Museum is this place, which exhibits
traditional Bulgarian costumes and mock-ups of traditional homes.
🅐 ul Vitosha 3 🕕 0579 72177 🅦 http://museumbalchik.com
🕒 08.00–12.00, 13.00–16.30 Mon–Fri 🅘 Admission charge

🔺 Balchik's Royal Palace

Golf
The development boom of the mid- to late 2000s saw several golf courses get the green light, and visitors to the area can now putt and swing to their hearts' content. Try **Black Sea Rama** (W www.blacksearama.com) or **Lighthouse Golf Resort** (W http://lighthousegolfresort.com), both of which are in the vicinity of Balchik.

Izkustvo Galerija (Art Gallery)
Balchik's art gallery hosts a small display of religious icons from the area, but it's worth the visit as much for the view from outside. Standing on the terrace in front of the large white building, you look out over a delightful yellow church and its bell tower.
ⓐ ul Otets Paissii 4 ⓣ 0879 998 946 Ⓦ http://museumbalchik.com
ⓔ gallery@balchik.net Ⓛ 09.00–12.00, 13.00–16.00 Mon–Fri, closed Sat & Sun ❶ Admission charge

Istoricheski Muzei (Municipal Historical Museum)
A short walk away from the art gallery is the Municipal Historical Museum, which displays mostly statues.
ⓐ pl Nezavisimost 1 ⓣ 0579 72177 Ⓦ http://museumbalchik.com
Ⓛ 08.00–12.00, 13.00–16.30 Mon–Fri, closed Sat & Sun
❶ Admission charge

AFTER DARK

Restaurants
Regina Maria ££ The over-sea terrace is the big draw at this beachside hotel eatery, which boasts plenty of decent seafood. ⓐ On the seafront ⓣ 0524 60069 Ⓦ www.reginamariaspa.com Ⓛ 07.30–24.00 daily

Valeo Hotel and Restaurant ££ Fine dining in a restaurant-bar that looks more like one of New York's trendiest new hangouts than a Bulgarian seaside eatery. ⓐ ul Samara 6 ⓣ 0579 77029 Ⓦ www.hotelvaleo.com
ⓔ hotelvaleo@gmail.com

Albena

Exclusive, fashionable and upmarket, Albena is as well equipped and efficient as Bulgarian coastal resorts come. One significant section of its clientele is German package tourists. Neither they nor the wealthy locals will put up with the vagaries of typical eastern European organisation, and consequently things run smoothly.

A distinct architectural style also sets the town apart from its peers. Eschewing the tall, straight communist-style structures that are typical of Bulgaria's hotels, many of Albena's guests lodge in pyramid-shaped hotels, reputedly designed for the rooms to have better light, and these buildings are among the most distinctive on the Black Sea coast.

It's not the cheapest of the resorts in the area, particularly for the food and drink, and you have to pay a small fee to park in the town. But costs are still some way below what you would expect to pay in an equivalent Western European retreat. What's more, the higher prices mean that Albena is not as overrun by tourists and is therefore not as built up as some of its neighbouring resorts.

Much of the town is pedestrianised and pleasantly green and lush, and the few roads that run through it are quiet and tree-lined. You are well advised to abandon your car and take in the sights on foot or, better yet, hop on one of the mini-trains on wheels that wind around the town. Don't bother looking for road names: it's a purpose-built resort and there are none.

Children are well catered for with an array of activities from donkey rides to mini-golf and buggy racing. Adults' needs are also met. The hotels are fully 21st century and accept credit cards; many of them even have Wi-Fi Internet access for those who just can't be out of the loop. Adrenalin junkies can try parasailing or other watersports, while the languid can simply soak up the sun or relax with a spa treatment.

There are no sites of historical interest to look around. Albena was wholly created over the past few decades with the tourist in mind. It's hedonism and holidaymaking, not history, that are what this resort is all about. More information is available at Ⓦ www.albena.bg

BEACHES

Thanks to Albena's exclusivity, its beach area is less cluttered than some of the coastline further up or down. It is possible to lie on the wide, white beach with the sea in front of you, the blue sky above and only trees behind, with no sign of the tourist shops to be found elsewhere.

The beach is dotted with straw umbrellas for when the heat gets too much. But there is far more than sunbathing on offer. The beach boasts a small football pitch with two decent-sized goals, a volleyball net and some climbing frames for children. Indeed, it's a good choice for families all round: it's upmarket, safe and clean, and the sea remains shallow for some way out, making it suitable for children's swimming.

THINGS TO SEE & DO

Excursions

Whether it's wine tasting, witnessing a mock wedding, dining at a folk restaurant or heading off in a 4x4 to explore the area and visit a traditional village, Albena provides the starting point. Tours are also available further afield, to other resorts, monasteries and even Romania.

Luna Park

The park, in the centre of town, offers mini-golf, a small buggy track and donkey rides, as well as pleasant gardens through which to have a wander, and well-placed benches to park yourself on.

Spa treatments

Lie back, relax and allow yourself to be pampered. Whether you want to bust your cellulite, slow down the ageing process or just relax and de-stress, medical and beauty experts are on hand to cater to your every whim. The hypothermic mineral water springs, kept at 30°C, are a particular draw to visitors.

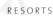

Tsentr Kultura (Cultural Centre)

Albena's cultural centre provides culture of every conceivable kind, hosting events from traditional Bulgarian song and dance displays and classical music nights featuring the works of Strauss and Brahms, to magic and exotic animal shows. Look for the adverts on its doors or posted around town for details. Top pop bands also perform here from time to time.

Watersports

Of course, most visitors to Albena expect to hit the waves at one time or another, whether that means having a gentle splash and a swim or indulging in some full-on extreme watersports. Waterskiing, parasailing, yachting, surfing, underwater fishing, jet-skiing, paragliding, sky-diving and scuba diving through PADI are all on offer from the half a dozen or so sports centres on the beach. Tennis, football, riding and fitness clubs are also available for those who like their sports a little less terrifying.

AFTER DARK

Dining out in Albena can be a costly business. If you're staying in the resort it is unavoidable, but if you're just passing through it's worth eating before or after. Restaurants here tend to open and close frequently, so it's difficult to give accurate listings. Staff at your hotel should be able to point you in the right direction, or ask other tourists for recommendations.

Restaurants

Rai ££ The nightly folklore show is the big draw at this beachside place. The fare is mostly meat, with chicken and veal the favourites, but you can also get fish and salad. ⓐ By the beach 🕐 09.00–24.00 daily

Blue Sky £££ For a great view of the coast, head up to the 17th-floor terrace at the top of the Dobrudja Hotel. It's a smart place, the food is decent and the service excellent. ⓐ Dobrudja Hotel 🕿 0579 62020 🕐 07.30–10.00, 12.30–14.00, 18.30–21.00 daily (summer only)

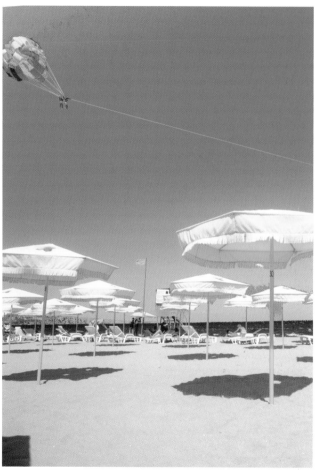

● *Parasailing and parasols at Albena*

Golden Sands

0 — 500 metres
0 — 500 yards

Albena

Amphitheatre

Berlin
Hotel

Yacht
Port

Lilia Hotel

Kaliakra Palace
Hotel

Varna

Black
Sea

Madara
Hotel

④ ⑤
Admiral Hotel
⑩

⑨ Vladislav
Hotel
①

International
Hotel

Harry's Diving Centre

③
⑦
⑥
⑧
Astera Hotel

Aquapolis
Water Park

Hotel Perunika ⑪

②
Hotel Kamchia

Preslav Hotel

St Constantine
& Elena

N

	Church
i	Information
	Police Station
	Bus Stop
	Post Office
	Shopping

Golden Sands

If a UK town had been shipped to Bulgaria and attached to the coast, Golden Sands would be it. Aside from the numerous British accents you will hear as you walk around, the shops and restaurants also advertise its Anglophile credentials. From tattoo and piercing parlours (with various comic variations on the spelling) and restaurants proudly proclaiming their full English breakfasts and British tea, to a plethora of clothes shops and stalls selling everything from sunglasses, wallets and beach gear to England flags, football shirts and tracksuit tops with celebrities' names branded across them, this resort truly is a home from home for the Brits. British and English flags bedeck business after business, from the most cheap and cheerful pub to the most upmarket hotel. For the really homesick, there are even a couple of McDonald's outlets.

Unlike its more sprawling counterpart in the southern resorts, Sunny Beach, Golden Sands is just about small enough to get around on foot. Much of its central strip is pedestrianised and dotted with bars, restaurants, nightclubs, seaside entertainment and market stalls, with the hotels set slightly further back from the seafront but still affording excellent views.

The streets in the resort do not have names and the buildings are not numbered, but it is not a difficult place to find your way around, with most of the attractions on or very close to the main strip. For unwilling walkers, a wheeled train will take you around the resort for a small sum. The emphasis is on fun and entertainment, and Golden Sands sometimes feels a bit like a fairground – an idea that is reinforced by its large beach Ferris wheel.

BEACHES

It's easy to see why so many tourists flock here. Golden Sands got its name for a reason – a beautiful, 5 km (3-mile) stretch of sand. The beach slopes gently and the sea has no cross-current, which makes it ideal for swimmers. Wide and clean with beautifully soft sand, it suits the active and inactive alike. The resort has pretty much every beach activity it's possible to think of, from volleyball and scuba diving for the energetic to on-beach massage for those who just want to indulge themselves and be totally spoiled.

With an inexpensive mini-golf green and small beachfront race track, there is plenty to occupy children, most of whom will be keen to try out the large Ferris wheel that dominates the Golden Sands skyline and serves as a useful orientation point. The small boating lake – a version of dodgems on water – is also popular with children.

Parts of the beach are fenced off for private use and some areas charge a fee – look for the signs. Typically you will be charged if you sit among the umbrellas, while in front or behind them is free, public space. To sit on a mattress costs around 6 leva, renting a sunbed or umbrella roughly double that.

THINGS TO SEE & DO

Aquapolis Water Park

With slides and pools for both adults and children, a whirlpool and several eating options, this is a good alternative to the beach, particularly if the weather is bad. It's not cheap by Bulgarian standards – prices are based on height so be prepared to shell out if you have a tall family – but your entrance fee includes use of the inflatables and there's a discount after 16.00.

ⓐ On the road to Albena ⓣ 0523 89966 ⓦ www.aquapolis.net
ⓔ aquapolis@goldensands-bg.com ⓛ 10.00–19.00 daily (summer)
ⓘ Admission charge

Casinos

As ubiquitous here as estate agents and fashion stores, casinos can be spotted fairly frequently at Golden Sands and elsewhere, with most hotels having their own casino on the premises. Make sure everyone in your group takes their passport if you go, as each person must register before being admitted.

Scuba diving

Harry's Diving Centre meets all your sub-aquatic needs, whether you fancy seeing some archaeological sites on the seabed, doing a spot of underwater fishing or just want to learn the ropes. Boats go out to diving spots at Golden Sands, Cape Kaliakra and Cape Shabla. The centre offers PADI and SSI courses.

ⓐ Just off the central beach, close to the post office ☎ 0523 56701, 0893 327744 ⓦ http://divewithharry.com ⏰ 10.00–19.00 (May–Oct)

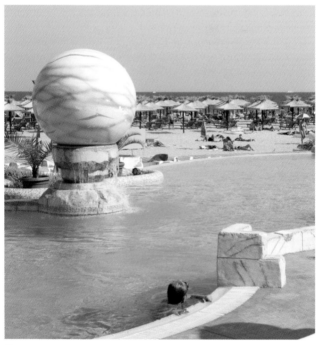

🔺 *Cooling down in the beachside pool*

TAKING A BREAK

Golden Sands has an array of budget restaurants, all with the tourist in mind. Because the resort is large and self-contained, there is tight competition for your business, and prices vary little from one place to another – with one or two luxury exceptions. Most places that are suitable for taking a break in the day also do main meals at night, so they are listed together.

Ivan's Place £ ❶   An institution on the Golden Sands scene, lively Ivan's has them coming back again and again. There's a football theme to the place with big matches shown on TV screens, and karaoke. A warm welcome and efficient service await. ⓐ Near Vladislav Hotel ❶ 0887 277874 ⓛ 08.00–23.30 daily

Izbata £ ❷   A well-liked restaurant serving mostly meaty, Bulgarian cuisine, though there's also a children's menu. A live band adds to the jollity. ⓐ Hotel Kamchia ❶ 0898 773403 ⓛ 11.30–23.00 daily

Mega Park Restaurant £ ❸   Unpretentious national cuisine served in a large room with a nautical motif; a fishing boat hangs suspended above your heads. They have a non-smoking room. ⓐ Next to Astera Hotel ❶ 0523 55723 ⓦ http://goldstrand-megapark.com ⓔ savadaritkov@gmail.com ⓛ 10.00–24.00 (summer only) ❶ Cash only

Gibraltar ££ ❹   Though it's not very well promoted or advertised, tourists repeatedly recommend this snack bar/restaurant for the standard of its food. You get great value for money and often some of the wine or beer accompanying your meal is thrown in for free. ⓐ Next to Admiral Hotel ❶ 0898 544304 ⓛ 10.30–23.30 daily

Shisha Bar ££ ❺   Belly dancers, hanging beads and veils are all part of the fun at this Arab-themed eatery – along with the obligatory smoking pipe, of course. ⓐ Next to Admiral Hotel ❶ 0898 578109 ⓛ 07.00–01.00 daily

⬥ *The name 'Golden Sands' describes the resort perfectly*

Silver Gourmet £££ ❻   Gourmet food in a fabulously chic restaurant, done out in smart grey and white. Deer and duck dishes are among the many treats that will tempt *bons viveurs*. ⓐ Astera Hotel
❶ 0523 597 90 Ⓦ www.silvergourmet.com ❶ 11.00–23.00

AFTER DARK

Bars & clubs

Arrogance Music Factory ❼   Stylish lounge and club where you can listen to house, pop folk, retro pop or chill-out music as the mood takes you, in one of the four different rooms. ⓐ Astera Hotel Casino
❶ 0885 800 275 Ⓦ www.arroganceclub.com ❶ 22.30–06.00
❶ Admission charge

Bonkers Disco ❽   Disco, house, Latino and oldies are on the playlist at this packed-out disco. ⓐ Next to the Astera Hotel ❶ 22.00–05.00
❶ Admission charge

Club Masai ❾   With an African name and interior, this house and dance club is an occasional venue for international DJs. ⓐ Behind Vladislav Hotel ❶ 22.00–late ❶ Admission charge

Den Glade Viking ❿   As risqué and raucous as its Viking theme suggests, this party pub is strictly for the young, up-for-it crowd.
ⓐ Next to the Eiffel Tower ❶ 0896 758151 Ⓦ www.dengladeviking.eu
❶ 22.00–05.00

Muppet Karaoke Bar ⓫   Hugely popular seaside singalong joint with drinks offers most nights. ⓐ Hotel Perunika ❶ 0523 55310
Ⓦ www.muppetbar.com ⓔ contactcs@muppetbar.com ❶ 20.00 or
21.00–06.00 or 08.00

St Constantine and Elena

Verdant and compact, St Constantine and Elena feels more like a park than a commercial holiday resort. The oldest resort along Bulgaria's Black Sea coast, it was started over 100 years ago. It was originally intended to host hospital patients, which may be the reason for the tranquil atmosphere it enjoys today, particularly in comparison to the bustling Golden Sands and Varna, its immediate neighbours to the north and south along the coast road.

It also differs from the other resorts in not having one main strip of shops along the beach, so lacks the buzz of some nearby places. This makes it suitable for older couples who are after a bit of peace and quiet, and who are willing to pay a bit more for the privilege. Varna is easily accessible by car or bus, so staying in St Constantine and Elena does not mean you will be cut off from the amenities of a large town.

BEACHES

St Constantine and Elena's small, relatively crowd-free beach can make a welcome change after the teeming Golden Sands. The surf at times gets a little rough, which deters swimmers, and watersports enthusiasts also go elsewhere, which preserves the calm of the beach for reading, sunbathing and relaxing. Its rocky areas and small pier make for picturesque photos. Unlike other beaches along the coast, it is divided into sections by a series of rocky patches, which affords a greater sense of privacy.

THINGS TO SEE & DO

Sports

Although far smaller and less developed than its surrounding resorts, there is still plenty in the way of physical activity in St Constantine and Elena. Scuba diving, go-karting, fishing and scooter rental are all options,

⬣ The beach at St Constantine and Elena

the latter being a good way to get around the town, particularly as there are not too many cars about. Tennis courts are also available.

TAKING A BREAK

Perhaps because of its small size, St Constantine and Elena is not well served for restaurants, and the places you do find tend to be on the pricey side. For this reason, tourists often head to nearby Varna for dinner. However, it is possible to get a decent-value meal.

Kopitoto ££ A gamut of old-school Bulgarian dishes present themselves at traditional Kopitoto, whose name means 'the hoof' (encapsulated in the hoof-style entrance and cow bells that adorn the interior). Unlike many Black Sea coast eateries, it's open year-round.
ⓐ Close to main bus stop at resort entrance ⓣ 0529 88768
ⓦ http://kopitoto.net ⓛ 10.30–24.00 daily

Dolce Vita £££ Pleasant garden restaurant serving up Italian cuisine, with decent and good-value pizza and pasta options. Wash down your meal with a bottle of Italian or local wine. The hotel also boasts a top fish restaurant. ⓐ Grand Hotel Varna ⓣ 0523 61491
ⓦ www.grandhotelvarna.com

Varna

Varna has truly embraced the foreign influx of tourists and property hunters who have made their way to Bulgaria's Black Sea coast. The town has become something of a hub and it is likely to be your first port of call when visiting any of the resorts in the northern cluster. Both a resort and a flourishing city in its own right, Varna has the charm of a holiday destination and all the modern comforts of a busy town, such as great shops and fantastic food.

In some ways, Varna almost feels like home. The names that you're used to seeing on your local high street – Benetton, Mango – are here, along with several high-class designer stores. In the swish shops of this city it's certainly difficult to see any traces of the communist regime that fell over two decades ago. Another unavoidable symbol is the Union Jack, usually heralding an estate agent catering to the many Brits who want to make the Black Sea coast their second home.

Despite its size, many of Varna's highlights can be seen on foot. Indeed, in the heart of the city there is no other way: the central area, leading up to the impressive cathedral, is pedestrianised, giving it a peaceful, relaxed ambience that belies the town's status as a thriving port and business centre. Fountains and small, well-tended gardens add to the effect. This traffic-free zone is brimming with cafés and restaurants, almost all of which have outside terraces that make great spots for people-watching.

THINGS TO SEE & DO

Arheologiceski Muzei (Archaeological Museum)
Housed in an atmospheric former school set in some gardens, like the town's art gallery, this place features religious icons as well as artefacts throughout several rooms.

ⓐ Mariya Luiza 41, on corner with bul Slivnitsa ⓣ 0526 81011
ⓦ www.amvarna.com ⓛ 10.00–17.00 Tues–Sun, closed Mon (summer); 10.00–17.00 Tues–Sat, closed Sun & Mon (winter)
ⓘ Admission charge

33

◒ The Archaeological Museum, once a girl's high school

Festa Dolphinarium

Aquatic fun for the children. Catch one of the half-hour displays of juggling, dancing and acrobatics from the most popular sea creature.

ⓐ Sea Gardens ❶ 0523 02199 ⓦ www.dolphinarium.festa.bg
🕒 Shows at 10.30, 12.00, 15.30 Tues–Sun, closed Mon (summer only)
❶ Admission charge

Gradska Hudozhestvena Galerija Boris Georgiev (Boris Georgiev City Art Gallery)

Round the back of the Methodist Church, the gallery displays mainly modern art, from traditional interwar paintings, sculptures and portraits to more contemporary Pop-Art-style exhibits. Upstairs houses the permanent exhibition, with works by both international and Bulgarian artists. Downstairs is the guest exhibition, with pieces that can be yours to take away for anything from 100 to 1,000 leva.

ⓐ Lyuben Karavelov 1 ❶ 0526 12363 🕒 10.00–17.00 Tues–Sun, closed Mon
❶ Admission charge

Katedrala na Opredelitelen Ulen Prisvoyavane (Cathedral of the Assumption)

Probably Varna's best-known piece of architecture, the 19th-century cathedral is equally impressive inside, with its ornate gold carvings, icons and throne. Outside is a small collection of stalls where old women knit and sell simultaneously. Babies' bootees and socks seem to be the main merchandise on offer, but the larger marketplace across the street has a far wider range, from fruit, vegetables and spices to wallets, soft toys and Russian dolls of political figures.

ⓐ pl Mitropolit Simeon ❶ 0526 13005 🕒 06.00–22.00 daily

TAKING A BREAK

Restaurants & cafés

Happy Bar & Grill £ ❶ Superb cheap-and-cheerful American-style diner chain that is brightly decorated with musical instruments and film

memorabilia. Great food and upbeat atmosphere. ⓐ ul Preslav 11
ⓣ 0526 02541 ⓔ office@happy.bg ⓛ 08.00–24.00 daily

Montrey ££ ❷ Large café-restaurant overlooking Varna's central
precinct, ideal for relaxing and watching the world go by. Follow a
sandwich, salad, pizza or pasta with one of their tempting desserts.
ⓐ ul Preslav 42 ⓣ 0526 02418 ⓛ 07.00–23.00 daily ⓘ Cash only

🔺 *Watch dolphins display their talents at the Festa Dolphinarium*

AFTER DARK

Restaurants

Chuchura ££ ❸ For a taste of traditional Bulgaria that has nothing to do with tourist trails or property booms, this is the place. From the folk costumes and tapestry on the walls to the food on your plate, this is home cooking through and through. ⓐ ul Dragoman 11 ❶ 0889 213519 ❶ 11.00–24.00

Dragoman Bistro ££ ❹ Lamb and rabbit dishes feature among the Bulgarian, Italian and international options on offer, with a wide range of wines to choose from to help wash them down. A fireplace adds ambience inside, and there are some tables outside. ⓐ ul Dragoman 43 ❶ 0526 21688 ❶ 08.30–23.00

Kashtata sas Slanceto ££ ❺ Fish specialities and veal are among the top attractions at this international themed place, not to mention its large, leafy terrace. ⓐ ul Tsar Asen 3 ❶ 0526 00181 ❶ 10.00–24.00 ❶ Cash only

Panorama restaurant ££ ❻ While the food is fairly standard meat-based Bulgarian cuisine, this restaurant, on the top floor of the Cherno More Hotel, is worth visiting for the spectacular view of the city alone. ⓐ bul Slivnitsa 33 ❶ 0526 12235 ⓦ www.en.chernomorebg.com ❶ 11.00–23.00 ❶ Cash only

Za Priateli ££ ❼ The name means 'For Friends', and with its budget prices and unfussy atmosphere, this pizzeria is a good place to come in a group. ⓐ ul Makedonia 82 ❶ 0526 02898, 0885 166390 ⓦ www.zapriateli.com ❶ 11.00–23.00

Capitol £££ ❽ This classy restaurant limits itself to a few, very well-executed dishes. The European cuisine is complemented by a wide range of Bulgarian and international wine, all served in a sophisticated dining

atmosphere. ⓐ ul Petko Karavelov 40 ⓣ 0526 88000 ⓦ www.capitol.bg
ⓔ office@capitol.bg ⓛ 10.00–24.00

Musala £££ ❾   Quite possibly Varna's best restaurant. Exemplary
service, delightful gourmet food and a classic Baroque interior make
dining here a rare pleasure. VIPs eat here and it is easy to see why. Highly
recommended. ⓐ Grand Hotel London, pl Musala 3 ⓣ 0526 64100
ⓦ www.londonhotel.bg ⓛ 07.00–10.00, 12.00–14.30, 19.00–23.00

Theatre
Varna Opera Theatre ❿   Opened in 1947, Varna's unmistakable pink
theatre hosts several shows a week, including opera, classical, rock and
popular music plus ballet, all at bargain prices. ⓐ pl Nezavisimost
ⓣ 0526 65010 ⓦ www.operavarna.bg ⓔ director@operavarna.bg

Bars & clubs
4as Pik ⓫   Dimly lit nightspot where the resident DJ plays a mixture
of pop, retro and Balkan music. ⓐ Coastal Avenue ⓣ 0899 842996,
0884 949100 ⓦ www.4aspik.com ⓛ 22.00–06.00 ⓘ Admission charge

Boogaloo ⓬   Quirky dive bar playing, rock, reggae and jazz. ⓐ bul Knyaz
Boris I 24 ⓣ 0896 540468 ⓛ 20.00–04.00

O'Neills ⓭   Varna has not escaped the global proliferation of
Irish pubs. Listen to live performances from Bulgarian, American
and Irish musicians as you sup your pint of the black stuff or your
whiskey. ⓐ bul Slivnitsa 33 ⓣ 0526 14586 ⓦ www.oneillsinvarna.com
ⓛ 11.00–late

Royal Classic ⓮   Intimate piano and live music bar, with veteran acts
and up-and-coming musicians all taking their turn at tinkling the ivories.
ⓐ ul Shipka 18 ⓣ 0526 01596 ⓛ 22.00–03.00
ⓘ Admission charge

Sunny Beach

For pure pleasure-seekers, Sunny Beach is a purpose-built paradise. The largest Black Sea coastal resort, it is made up almost entirely of hotels, restaurants and entertainment facilities, all geared to the convenience of the holidaymaker. Whether you've come on holiday for the thrills of watersports, to party until dawn in thumping nightspots or just to lie on one of the most beautiful stretches of sand on the coast, Sunny Beach obliges you. This is what makes it such a good choice for family groups: while there is plenty to keep children entertained, like special pools, slides, bouncy castles and mini-golf, adults are also well catered for.

As it is the biggest resort on the Black Sea coast, if you want to explore the whole town you really need a car. But the bus service runs until around 23.00, and in truth there's little need to see everything. Sunny Beach has so many hotels, restaurants, discos and beach activities that, wherever you are based, you are likely to be within easy reach of everything the sunseeker needs. The main action is centred on a 1.5 km-(1-mile) long pedestrianised strip full of eating and drinking options, as well as various market stalls. If you do want to go further afield you can hire a bicycle to get around, or even let someone else do the work by taking a rickshaw ride or the mini-train.

In the unlikely event that you do run out of things to occupy yourself, or if you just fancy seeing a bit more of the country, you're well placed to do so. Because Sunny Beach is so geared towards tourists, many visitors choose to use it as a base from which to travel around various parts of Bulgaria. Trips by bus and boat are available not only to the resorts in the vicinity, but also further afield to Sofia, Plovdiv and Varna among other places, which means that in between lapping up the sun you can take in your fair share of culture – museums, cities and monasteries.

BEACHES

Sunny Beach did not get its name for nothing. The sun seems to shine even when the rest of the country gets rain. The wide beach stretches off

Sunny Beach

0 — 60 metres

0 — 60 yards

Hotel Venera

Hotel Globus

Bor Hotel

Hotel Hrizantema

Lyulyak Hotel

Bar-Variety

Meridian Hotel

Pomorie Hotel

Sozopol Hotel

Black Sea

Kontinental Hotel

Bourgas, Nessebar

Hotel Fregata

N

Bus Stop
Post Office
Shopping

towards the cliffs in the distance – kilometre after kilometre of soft, grainy sand, perfect for long walks. Clean and safe, the beach is a worthy winner of the Blue Flag award. There is no shortage of other pursuits, such as fishing, volleyball and a wealth of watersports. Waterskiing, parasailing, hang-gliding, plus boat trips from banana boats and pedalos to yachts – it's difficult to think of a beach activity that isn't on offer. While some small businesses have set up on the beach, there are too few for it to feel cluttered or overly commercial.

Because the beach faces east, early birds can watch the sun rise over the warm sea, with the cliffs off to the left. With its rare sand dunes and as the habitat of several protected species of plant, Sunny Beach also has plenty to interest nature lovers.

Thanks to the mountains, which form a picturesque backdrop to the far left end of the beach as you look out to sea, the resort gets a fresh breeze that keeps sunbathers from overheating. The sea is warm, gentle and safe, with no unpredictable tides or nasty surprises like jellyfish. A flag system is in operation to indicate how safe it is to swim: green means fine for everyone, yellow indicates that only competent swimmers should go in the water and red prohibits swimming altogether.

Of course, with so much to recommend it, Sunny Beach does see large numbers of tourists. While that makes for a great atmosphere in the bars and discos long after the sun has gone down, it can be less welcome when you're trying to find a spot on the sand. For a bit more privacy and space, walk a little way north along the beach. The majority of hotels are concentrated in the south, which is why the southern part of the beach can fill up quicker.

THINGS TO SEE & DO

Watersports

As a beacon in the area for adrenalin junkies, it would almost be quicker to list the watersports that you can't do at Sunny Beach. Surfing, waterskiing, parasailing, hang-gliding and scuba diving are all on offer, and you can hit the waves in anything from a banana or rowing boat to a chartered yacht. The bonus is that the most extravagant water-based pursuit is still a bargain compared to what you'd be paying at an equivalent Western European resort.

�â– *Stay on your toes with beach volleyball*

AFTER DARK

Restaurants & cafés

Sunny Beach is entirely dedicated to summer season tourists. The season runs from around May to early October, when many places begin to close for the winter.

Bar and Food £ ❶ Obliging service and great value abound at this eatery, whose unassuming façade belies the smart swimming pool at the back. Pizza and pasta feature among a multitude of dishes, all of which punch above their weight, price-wise. There's also Wi-Fi Internet. ⓐ Opposite Hotel Globus, next to Royal Beach Mall ⏱ 09.00–24.00

China House £ ❷ Red lanterns herald your arrival at China House, a well-recommended restaurant that does exactly what it says on the tin. ⓐ Hotel Venera, behind Hotel Globus ☏ 0899 890138

The Corner Pub ££ ❸ Part of the Meridian Hotel, this huge pub is also a restaurant, serving English and international cuisine from fish specials, grilled meat and roast dinners to spaghetti bolognese. With its pool table, football shirts and flags, plus large screen and Sky TV, it's a favourite among tourists. ⓐ Meridian Hotel ☏ 0888 403107 ⏱ 08.30–last customer ❶ Cash only

Red Lion ££ ❹ Unashamedly British pub – as the name suggests – with pool, darts, big screens, live music, karaoke, bingo and a quiz night. ⓐ Royal Beach Mall ⓦ http://redlionpub.eu ⓔ redlionpub@gmail.com ⏱ 09.30–02.00

Bars & clubs

Elephant ❺ Set as it is in a tent, and with its name, you could almost be in India rather than eastern Europe. Unusual beachfront club that delivers something a bit different. ⓐ Cacao Beach ☏ 0888 639035 ⓦ www.elephant.kvartira.bg/den.html

Lazur ❻ One of the big names on the scene, Lazur has built up a loyal fan base over its 40-year-plus history. Two floors, 12 bars, a pool and a garden should keep you entertained for a while. ⓐ Opposite Pomorie Hotel ⓦ www.discoclublazur.com ⓔ discolazur@gmail.com ⓛ 22.00–06.00 ❶ Admission charge

Makalali ❼ African-themed nightclub with big zebra-print sofas, drapes and pine decorations. By day it operates as a relaxing chill-out zone, at night a DJ spins house, retro and commercial tunes. ⓐ Behind Globus Hotel ⓔ makalali_club@mail.bg

⬥ Sunny Beach's shopping streets offer plenty of distractions

Nessebar

It's easy to see why Nessebar (sometimes written as Nessebur, or other variations) is a UNESCO-protected site. It has retained not only many remnants of its history, but also its atmosphere of a picturesque fishing village. Famous as much for its 19th-century wooden architecture as for its cluster of small medieval churches, it feels a world away from the more commercial resorts, and its relative isolation has served it well. The old town is almost like an island, set on a peninsula connected to nearby Sunny Beach by one main road, which means that you rarely have to walk more than a minute or so before you're confronted with dazzling blue sea. It's a small settlement, entirely navigable on foot, and indeed many areas are almost entirely car free, which only adds to its island charm.

Although Nessebar is by no means lacking in the facilities that the visitor needs, such as hotels, restaurants, museums and souvenir shops, it has a markedly different feel from its larger neighbour. While Sunny Beach is modern, large and purpose-built, Nessebar has grown naturally and organically, its small size protecting it from the excesses of developers. That's not to say it's entirely uncommercialised: Nessebar's obvious charm brings tourists in droves.

The two main draws are fish and history. Little boats line the shore and the plethora of tempting fish restaurants that look out to the sea serve the day's catch. There are many places where you can take a seat and watch the town's fishermen going about their work. Anywhere you wander, you'll be surrounded by a sense of the island's past. Whether it's the remnants of historical ruins and old churches, the timeless craft of the fishermen or the absence of huge hotels, in Nessebar the 21st century feels far away.

BEACHES

Some visitors rate Nessebar's beaches as the best in Bulgaria – with it being a peninsula, the beachgoer is spoilt for choice. Owing to the town's popularity, its vast stretch of fine golden sand can get crowded,

Nessebar Bay

Black Sea

Customs

Arheologiceski Muzei

Etnografski Muzei

HAN ASPAROUH
GLAROUS
EDELVAIS
MITROPOLITSKA
SLAVIANSKA
HEMOUS
HEMOUS
TERVEL
AHELOI
HAN ALEXANDER
RIBARSKA
TSAR SIMEON
MENA
CHAIKA
MESSAMBRIA
MITROPOLITSKA
AHELOI
TEIR
KRAILCHENKA
SEVERA
VIHREN
NEPTUN
KRAIBREJNA
SADIA
SLAVIANSKA
HIONA
AVKORA
NEPTUN
VENERA
MESSAMBRIA

Sunny Beach
Bourgas

Nessebar

0 — 100 metres
0 — 100 yards

Church
Bus Stop
Post Office
Shopping

N

particularly later in the morning when the day-trippers begin to pile in. Some visitors recommend the beach area in the new town.

For watersports, most people head to nearby Sunny Beach. One of the main pleasures of Nessebar's seashore is watching the fishermen at work, and the small boats bobbing in the harbour.

THINGS TO SEE & DO

Arheologiceski Muzei (Archaeological Museum)
Appropriately set among some of the town's ruins, the museum houses stone carvings, masks, statues, urns, coins, jewellery and anchors, many of which are over 2,000 years old. Downstairs there is a collection of icons.
ⓐ Inside the old town gateway ⓣ 0554 46019/2 ⓦ www.ancient-nessebar.com ⓛ 09.00–19.00 Mon–Fri, 09.00–13.30, 14.00–18.00 Sat & Sun

Churches
Anyone who enjoys church architecture will be in their element in Nessebar. Built over the centuries, the various styles reflect the influences of whichever group was in power at the time. Ceramics and frescoes are some of the highlights.

Etnografski Muzei (Ethnographical Museum)
This small museum contains examples of the national dress and other curiosities.
ⓐ ul Mesembria 28 ⓣ 0554 46012 ⓛ 10.00–13.00, 14.00–18.00 Tues–Sat; closed Sun & Mon ⓘ Admission charge

TAKING A BREAK

Klio ice cream parlour ££ ❶ If you like your sundaes accompanied by loud dance music, try sitting inside Klio. If you prefer peace and quiet, choose one of the outside tables overlooking the sea. ⓐ By the Archaeological Museum ⓣ 0878 192072 ⓛ 09.00–24.00 daily

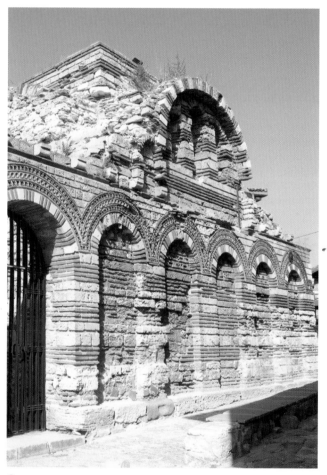

◔ *Nessebar has some fine examples of Byzantine architecture*

AFTER DARK

Restaurants

There is a cluster of restaurants at the point where you enter the town, by the bus stop. All have a sea view and tables outside. Have a walk around and you're bound to find something that suits you, and the competition means that prices are fairly standard. As you go further into Nessebar, the next main eating area is around the Ethnographical Museum. It's a small resort, so credit card acceptance is improving but not yet universal.

Captain Nemo ££ ❷ Occupying a superb spot overlooking the bay, the views are matched by excellent fresh seafood. Sit outside to enjoy both to the maximum. ⓐ ul Kralbrezhna 18A ☎ 0878 688333 🕒 12.00–15.00, 18.00–24.00 daily

Flagman ££ ❸ Fish restaurant serving up almost anything that swims – salmon, shark, blue fish, scad and crayfish are all on the menu, and there is a tank of live crabs from which to select your dinner if you want ultimate freshness. Other cosmopolitan treats such as blue cheese salad also mark this place out from the competition. ⓐ By the bus stop 🕒 09.00–21.00 daily

Kapitanska Sreshta ££ ❹ A charming fish restaurant in what is possibly the best location on the island, as well as being the oldest house. A big keg, fishing boat and three model drunken sailors liven the place up. The extensive menu features salmon, octopus, mussels and crab. ⓐ By the Ethnographical Museum ☎ 0554 42124 🕒 10.00–around 23.00 daily ❗ Cash only

Mehana Pri Shopite ££ ❺ Atmosphere and food both score top marks at this genial restaurant, the centrepiece of which is a centuries-old fig tree. ⓐ ul Neptoun 12 ☎ 0888 434440 🕒 11.00–24.00 daily

Sevina ££ Glass-fronted restaurant overlooking the sea, where you can munch on salads, seafood or national dishes while sipping a cocktail or two. Its nearby sister restaurant is Zornitza. ⓐ ul Messambria, next to Community Centre ⓣ 0554 44873 ⓦ www.zornitza.info ⓔ zornitza_nessebar@abv.bg ⓛ 08.00–01.00 daily

Bars & clubs
Xtreme ❼ Lounge-style club playing house, retro and commercial tracks. ⓐ ul Han Krum 11 ⓣ 0897 844866/7 ⓛ 08.00–late daily

● Seafood restaurants are excellent and plentiful

Pomorie

Pomorie is nestled between the sea on one side and Lake Pomorie on the other. Lake Pomorie is a salt lagoon that is famous in the area for its 2,000-year-old mud treatments and also for its excellent birdwatching opportunities.

Despite its small size, the town has a sophisticated social scene and nightlife. As such, it would suit couples who want to escape the tourist hordes without giving up a decent choice of restaurants and bars. High-quality grapes grow in the region, so trying the local wine is certainly something to put on your to-do list. The main places to eat, drink and dance are in or around the pedestrianised area ul Knyaz Boris, which is marked by the **Church of the Nativity**.

BEACH

Not being a major resort, Pomorie's beach can provide some welcome space and privacy in high season. The water is shallow and therefore suitable for all swimmers. Wooden barriers have been constructed to prevent sea erosion. There's a pier where aspiring fishermen try their luck.

THINGS TO SEE & DO

Birdwatching
Pomorie Lake, by the Salt Museum, is a top spot for twitchers, and conservationists have made great strides in breeding and protection. From six pairs of nesting terns in 1996, the number had surpassed 1,000 within a decade. Over 240 species of birds frequent the area, several of which are threatened throughout the world.

Musej na Solta (Salt Museum)
Dedicated to the area's main product, this quirky little museum explains how salt production technology has developed from ancient times and

features videos in English, old photos and live demonstrations.
ⓐ Behind the stadium ☏ 0596 25344, 0887 377110 ✉ alas@unacs.bg
🕐 08.00–18.00 Mon–Sat, closed Sun (summer); 10.00–14.30 Mon–Fri,
closed Sat & Sun (winter) ❶ Admission charge

St Rojdestvo Bogorodichno (Church of the Nativity)
This is the town's central church, which is much more cavernous inside
than it appears from the outside. With its candles and chanting, it is dark
and particularly atmospheric.
ⓐ ul Knyaz Boris 🕐 07.00–13.00, 15.30–18.00

AFTER DARK

Restaurants & cafés
Paradise Café ££ Trendy orange café, serving coffees, milkshakes, cocktails
and desserts to Pomorie's smart set. ⓐ Opposite the Church of the
Nativity 🕐 07.00–24.00 daily

St George ££ Traditional and upmarket hotel restaurant, done out in an
English style with photos on the walls. Serves veal, fish, pizza and pasta
in a classy, serene atmosphere. ⓐ ul Javarov 15 ☏ 0596 24411
🕐 08.00–24.00 daily ❶ Open year-round

Sozopol

Popular with artists and writers for over a hundred years, Sozopol is the top cultural spot of the southern group of Black Sea resorts. Its museums, galleries, art and music clubs, not forgetting a smattering of small, pretty churches, create an air of sophistication lacking in some of the more tourist-oriented resorts. Shoppers in Sozopol are more likely to be offered a portrait by one of the street artists than a replica football shirt. Concerts take place throughout the summer at the town's amphitheatre, and the same venue hosts the main event in Sozopol's cultural calendar, the Apollonia Festival.

A fishing village, the town is pretty with narrow, sloping, cobbled streets that wind between two-storey overhanging houses. Besides the hotels and restaurants that cater to the modern traveller, it's easy to imagine that very little else has changed over the years. A pleasant park commemorating the area's fallen soldiers adds to the sense of history.

BEACHES

Sozopol is made up of two main sections. On the mainland is the Harmanite area, an up-to-date district where you will find most of the hotels, as well as South or Harmanite Beach. It's the biggest stretch of sand in the town itself, so can be a better bet in the peak months of July and August. Lifeguards patrol the seafront; the sea has currents and can get rough at times. Keep an eye out for the red flag, which indicates that swimming is dangerous. Umbrellas and chairs are available for a small fee, and there's a separate area for everyone else. Topless, but not nude, sunbathing is permitted.

The Old Town is on the peninsula, which curves round to an easterly point, and here you'll find the popular Central Beach, which can get busy in high season. Like Harmanite Beach, there is a charge for the use of umbrellas and chairs, which have their own area. Again, topless sunbathing is permitted.

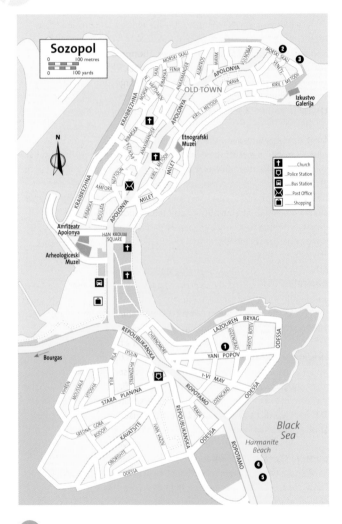

Sozopol

0	100 metres
0	100 yards

OLD TOWN

MORSKI SKALI
SKALI
MORSKI
RIBARSKA
FENIX
ALBATROS
MAVAK
APOLONYA
ANAKSIMANDER
DRAVA
MORSKI SKALI
VENEDS
KIRIL I METODII

Izkustvo
Galerija

KRAIBREZHNA
RIBARSKA
VAJMGAROV
MORSKI
RIBARSKA
ANAKSIMANDER
KIRIL I METODII
APOLONYA

Etnografski
Muzei

NEPTUN
KIRIL I METODII
MILET

AMFORA
KOLIATA
RIBARSKA
KRAIBREZHNA

APOLONYA
MILET

Amfiteatr
Apolonya

HAN KROUM
SQUARE

Arheologiceski
Muzei

← Bourgas

REPOUBLIKANSKA
CHERNOMORE
LYULIN
RILA
STRANDZHA
LAZOUREN
OVCHARKA
DERVENT
BRYAG
HRISTO BOTEV
ODESSA

YANI POPOV

VIHREN
MOUSSALA
VITOSHA
RILA
STARA PLANINA

1-VI MAY
ROPOTAMO
OVCHARKA
TRAKA
ODESSA

SREDNA GORA
RODOPI
KAVATSITE
YAN YAZOV
REPOUBLIKANSKA
ODESSA

OBORISHTE
ODESSA
ROPOTAMO

Black
Sea

Harmanite
Beach

Symbol	
✝	........Church
🚓	.Police Station
🚌	..Bus Station
✉	....Post Office
🛍	........Shopping

54

A third option exists for those who like a little more privacy. Three kilometres (2 miles) north of town is the Gold Fish campsite, which has a private beach, accessible for a small sum. There is also a charge for the use of an umbrella. Although not officially permitted, nude sunbathing is generally more acceptable here than at the two beaches in town.

THINGS TO SEE & DO

Amfiteatr Apolonya (Apollonia Amphitheatre)
While Sozopol's amphitheatre might have the feel of somewhere more ancient, it was in fact built relatively recently for the Apollonia Festival of Arts (see page 107). It also gets some use throughout the rest of the summer as a concert venue. The festival website hosts a comprehensive programme of events, including ticket details.
ⓐ By the Archaeological Museum and the library ☎ 0298 07833, 0550 22122 Ⓦ www.apollonia.bg

Arheologiceski Muzei (Archaeological Museum)
Pottery and pictures dating back over 2,000 years. Old anchors are among the more memorable exhibits.
ⓐ Khan Krum 2 ☎ 0550 22226 🕐 08.00–17.00 daily (summer); Mon–Fri 08.00–17.00 (winter) ❶ Admission charge

Etnografski Muzei (Ethnographical Museum)
Set among the remains of a well and a fortress wall and tower, the museum really feels steeped in history. Inside are old artefacts showcasing the town's past as a Greek colony and the fishing that has sustained it.
ⓐ Kiril i Metodii 34 ☎ 0550 22748 ⓔ office@sozopol-foundation.com 🕐 08.30–18.00 Mon–Fri, closed Sat & Sun ❶ Admission charge

Izkustvo Galerija (Art Gallery)
The fishing theme continues with historical and more contemporary art, housed in the town's former high school.
ⓐ Kiril i Metodii 70 🕐 10.00–19.30 Mon–Sat, closed Sun

◆ *Traditional housing in Sozopol*

AFTER DARK

Restaurants & cafés

Kavaler ££ ❶ Intimate eatery serving seafood, including indulgent treats like caviar. ⓐ ul Yani Popov 21 ❶ 0550 23646 ⓦ www.hotelkavaler.com ⓔ kavalerbg@abv.bg

Windmill ££ ❷ Popular Bulgarian restaurant with meat dishes that are set alight before your eyes, folk shows and dancing. ⓐ ul Morski Skali 27 ❶ 0550 22844 ⓔ wm.soz.bg@abv.bg ⓛ 10.30–24.00 daily

Di Valli £££ ❸ Trendy eatery serving up more adventurous fare than most of its competitors, with a Mediterranean twist. ⓐ ul Morski Skali 35 ❶ 0888 982265 ⓦ www.divalli.com ⓛ 10.00–24.00 daily

Bars & clubs

Club Cult ❹ Playing everything from retro classics to house, dance, soul and R&B, this place is worth a visit for the barmen doing their best impersonation of Tom Cruise in *Cocktail*. ⓐ Harmanite Beach ❶ 0888 563446 ❶ Admission charge

Havana ❺ Pizzeria and bar in one, famed for its wild dancing plus its patio and swimming pool. ⓐ Harmanite Beach ❶ 0888 452881 ⓛ 24 hours daily (summer)

Primorsko

With its combination of bustling nightspots and a wide range of water-based activities, Primorsko is ideal for young adults who want to wring every bit of fun out of their holiday, both day and night. It's not the most upmarket of resorts, but that attracts a young, fun-loving crowd, and Primorsko regulars rave about the wild clubs and cheap tequila.

BEACHES

With a grassy knoll running down to it and plenty of trees dotted around, Primorsko's beach has a natural, rough-hewn quality to it. At the northern end, the choppy sea attracts windsurfers, while the calmer waters in the southern part are better for swimmers. Primorsko's bargain prices do mean that the beaches can fill up quickly. Nearby options for those wanting a little more space are Perla beach, accessible by the small wheeled train, and the International Youth Centre, a hotel complex just 2 km (1 mile) south of the town. Watch out for a red flag, which means the water is too rough for swimming.

THINGS TO SEE & DO

Diving
Poseidon diving centre offers a range of aquatic activities in the nearby area.
ⓐ Kiril i Metodii 16 ⓣ 0888 935124 ⓦ http://poseidonbg.com
ⓔ lyubomir.velchev@gmail.com ⓛ morning dive at 08.30 or 09.00

AFTER DARK

Restaurants & cafés
The Old Mill ££ Large, simple eatery offering Bulgarian cuisine, sometimes accompanied by live music. ⓐ ul Treti Mart 50
ⓣ 0899 848747

Bars & clubs

Impulse A Primorsko favourite, Impulse attracts a young, up-for-it crowd. ⓐ ul Kostadinov

Luxor Gloriously tacky and hugely popular disco playing house, dance, retro and commercial tracks. Things can get rather raucous – it's not a place for wallflower types. ⓐ On the beach, look for the sphinx ⓣ 0896 655317 ⓘ Admission charge

🔺 *The church of Saint Stefan in Primorsko*

Ahtopol

If the seaside to you is nothing to do with jet skis, all-day English breakfasts and lilos, and more about tranquillity and traditional coastal activities like fishing, Ahtopol might be the place for you. A long way south of the main stretch of resorts clustered around Sunny Beach, it's only around 18 km (11 miles) from the Turkish border. But don't go expecting to see a huge outside influence; the town is isolated enough to have its own character that differs from its large neighbour or the usual effects of tourism. However, the town's somnolent atmosphere could change in the near future, as a large yacht marina has been mooted.

But for the moment at least, in Ahtopol, it is still possible to take a stroll and pass a donkey casually ambling the other way along the street. From the football pitch at the edge of town all the way to the beach, this is a place that has not been wholly subsumed by the tourist bug. Of course, there are hotels, restaurants and bars where a visitor can enjoy a drink or a meal while looking out to sea, but you won't see the usual shops of the more businesslike holiday resorts here.

Instead, you will find a small, self-contained town, which just happens to be by the sea and have some fantastic views of the rugged coastline. Anyone who does tire of the solitude and wants a taste of city life can book a trip out on one of the buses that serve Sofia and Bourgas several times a day.

BEACHES

Far from being packed with foreign tourists, your fellow beachgoers are more likely to be veteran fishermen just sitting and shooting the breeze. Set back from the beach is a pleasant and quiet park, popular with the old people of the town. But Ahtopol is not entirely conservative – the northern section of the beach is popular with nude bathers. If you do decide to bare all, make sure not to forget your wallet – there is a charge of a few leva for a sunshade.

◆ *Fishing boats at Ahtopol*

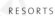

AFTER DARK

Restaurants & bars

Coloured House This unmistakable building (there can be no doubt as to how it got its name) is a convivial place to stop for a drink – the house is particularly proud of its home-made *rakia*. ⓐ ul Zelnika 7
ⓣ 0889 188328, 0884 153243 ⓦ www.moreto.biz

Eskada Beach £ Decorated in chic contemporary European style and boasting dramatic sea views, this relatively new hotel eatery has a terrace and a barbecue in the garden. The cuisine is Bulgarian with a few international staples. ⓐ G Kondolov 1 ⓣ 0550 62035, 0885 998502
ⓦ www.hoteleskada.com

Bar Grill ££ Bulgarian and Greek cuisine, including fish, roast lamb, pork or chicken and mussels. You can even take your meal on the beach itself.
ⓐ Lola Garden Hotel, ul Preobrazenska 7, Harmanite Beach
ⓣ 0887 000600 ⓦ www.lolagarden.com ⓛ 08.00–24.00 daily

○ *Flying high over the Black Sea*

EXCURSIONS
Out & about

A viewing platform overlooking Srebarna Nature Reserve

Excursions in the north

Srebarna Nature Reserve

Up near the Romanian border, a visit to Srebarna, though it might be off the beaten track, rewards both keen twitchers and any lovers of wide, open spaces. A large area of freshwater lake and marshland, adjacent to the River Danube, it is accessible by bus from the nearest town but is better seen by car if you want to get around the 600-hectare (1,483-acre) site. There are wildlife trails to follow, and it is also possible to take guided or solo tours. Once part of Romanian territory, the area has been a nature reserve for around 60 years and is on the UNESCO World Heritage list.

Top attraction has to be the birds. Almost 100 different species have made the lake their home, and another 80 pass through on what is called the Via Pontica, a migration route for birds between Europe and Africa. The Dalmatian pelican, great egret, night heron, purple heron, glossy ibis and white spoonbill are just a few of the treats awaiting ornithologists. There is something to be seen for most of the year, whether it is pelicans in the spring, egrets in summer or geese in winter. If you are brave, try climbing up one of the somewhat rickety viewing posts – and bring your binoculars.

But birds are not the only things that seek the protection of this remote area. There are believed to be 39 species of mammal, 21 types of reptile and amphibians, and 10 fish species also in the area, some of which are facing extinction outside it. The stuffed creatures in the small museum (see page 66) will not be to everyone's taste, but the facility does give further information on some of the species you might spot if you're lucky, and its staff can suggest the best way to see the area, which can be quite a challenge due to its size.

But even if you can't tell your bluethroat from your greylag goose, the reserve has a strong appeal. Walking the narrow tracks with a canopy of trees above your head, at times you can hear nothing but distant birdsong.

Srebarna Nature Reserve is to the north of the road between Silistra and Ruse, which runs alongside the Danube – look for signs to either Srebarna or Vetren, the nearby villages. From Silistra, which is 17 km (10½ miles) away, you can pick up bus 222 from the bus station, and the area is also served by buses travelling between Silistra and Ruse.

THINGS TO SEE & DO

Prirodonauchen Muzei (Natural History Museum)
While the stuffed exhibits may not appeal to all, the museum covers the area's wildlife fairly well and gives you a clue as to what you can expect to see on your visit.
Srebarna village, follow the signs 10.00–16.00 Mon–Fri, closed Sat & Sun

AFTER DARK

Kalimaritsa ££ Traditional, hearty meals are just the ticket after a day spent rambling or birdwatching in the reserve. ul Stratsin 17, Vetren 085 14554 www.housekalimaritsa.bg hotel_kalimaritsa@abv.bg

Kaliakra Nature Reserve

If you like your nature untamed and elemental, it's worth making the journey north to the Kaliakra Nature Reserve. Cape Kaliakra juts out into the sea some 49 km (30 miles) up the coast from Balchik, and is like another place and time from the bustling resorts that dot the country's Black Sea coastline. Getting there is not easy – you need to either drive yourself, go with an organised tour group from Balchik or other resorts in the area, or be prepared for a lot of walking. But those who go to the bother are rewarded with one of Bulgaria's most captivating wildernesses.

Get lucky, and from the cliff tops you may spot a bottlenose dolphin plying the sea below, or even a rare shag. The cape is also a must on the

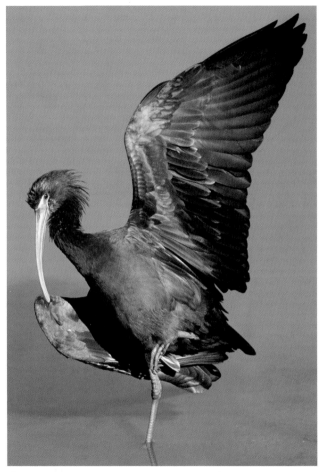

◆ *The glossy ibis is just one of the birds that visit Kaliakra*

BIRDWATCHING

Srebarna, the Bourgas Lakes, Cape Kaliakra and Pomorie are among the many excellent areas in Bulgaria for birdwatching. If you're new to twitching, here are a few tips to help get to you started.

Do your homework beforehand. Read up on what kind of birds you're likely to see – and that means reading the descriptions as well as looking at the pictures. Make sure you're well acquainted with any common species. Birds tend to be more active early in the day, particularly in warm weather, so it's worth setting the alarm and making an early start. Just before sunset is also a good time to spot some types.

The main thing is to have a decent pair of binoculars. It's worth buying the best you can, but there's no need to break the bank – a secondhand pair will do the job just as well. Listening is just as important as looking. Birdsong may be your first clue that a particular bird is in your area, and some birds are far more likely to reveal themselves by sound than by sight.

Understandably, the birds you might spot out in the wild will be less comfortable with your presence than the pigeons in your local park. Wear clothes that blend in with the natural environment, and that won't make a noise when you move. Conceal yourself by standing by a tree or in foliage. Keep your voice down and move around slowly.

Have patience. Even expert twitchers can struggle to recognise and place the birds they spot. Enjoy the experience and don't expect to master the skill straightaway. Finally, it goes without saying that you should interfere with the birds as little as possible – this is especially important when they are around their nests or with their young.

birdwatcher's list of places to go around the Black Sea coast, due to the ideal breeding conditions it affords. Whatever time of year you go, you should be able to spot birds of one kind or another. But even if you don't see any of the wildlife whose habitats are carefully preserved at the site, the reserve rewards your visit with the centuries-old ruins of churches, wells and castle walls, as well as its bracing, *Wuthering Heights*-style atmosphere. The cape's rural, desolate position was the very reason that it was chosen for the construction of Tirisis, an ancient fortress that was used by the various races ruling the area over the centuries.

Amble along the rustic, irregular pathways that run along the top of limestone rocks, around 60 to 70 m (200 to 230 ft) high, and you could just as easily be in the 1st century as the 21st century. Cars, trains, all modernity is forgotten as you get back to nature. Even the tourist market is largely of the traditional kind – the stall owners are usually knitting their products in between selling them. Charming lace tablecloths are also on sale.

ⓐ Cape Kaliakra ⓝ Driving, or booking an organised trip from your resort, is the easiest way to get to Kaliakra. The cape is 12 km (7½ miles) from Kavarna, from where you can take a public bus as far as Balgarevo, which still leaves you with a 6-km (4-mile) walk. Tour companies run buses from Kavarna and Balchik among other places ● 08.00–18.00 daily (May–Oct) ❶ Admission charge, payable at the booth on the approach road to the reserve

THINGS TO SEE & DO

Muzeum Kaliakra (Kaliakra Museum)
The restaurant area includes the entrance to the small museum. Housed in a cave in the side of the cliff face, it's a charming add-on, in keeping with the authentic feel of Kaliakra. As you enter, sounds of the sea, birds or battles quietly echo. In two small rooms are housed collections of pottery and jewellery from the medieval, Hellenic and Byzantine periods that give a brief insight into the area's colourful history.

⬣ *The dramatic limestone cliffs of Kaliakra*

Nature-spotting

Kaliakra is special mainly for the wildlife that makes its home there. The area is the habitat for over 240 rare and endangered animal and plant species.

TURBULENT TIMES AT THE CAPE

While today Kaliakra has a peace and serenity that provides a counterpoint to the busy seaside resorts, it was not always so tranquil. The setting has seen both warfare and tragic sacrifice in the course of its history and mythology.

The Battle of Cape Kaliakra saw the Russian fleet take on the Turks in 1791. Despite their fewer boats and inferior firepower, the Russians saw off the Ottoman attack and the Turks retreated to Istanbul. It was the last battle in a war that had dragged on for five years.

The most popular legend that has survived, probably because of the picture it paints of the noble Bulgarian character, surrounds the Ottoman Conquest of the 14th century. It is said that, rather than undergo forced conversion to Islam and other humiliations at the hands of the invading Turks, 40 Bulgarian women tied their hair together and jumped from the rocks at Kaliakra to their deaths into the Black Sea. The story is commemorated with an obelisk at the entrance to the site, called the Gate of the 40 Maidens.

It is also said that the cape was formed when St Nicholas, the patron saint of sailors, was attempting to escape the Turks, and God made the land longer and longer to aid his getaway.

And a third legend has it that one of Alexander the Great's successors, Lysimachus, also tried to escape to the cape after stealing the royal treasure. Unfortunately for him, the powers above looked less beneficently on his plight and he drowned in a storm.

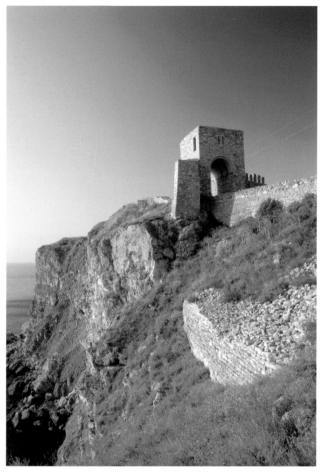

⬤ *The cliffs at Kaliakra provided an ideal site for fortifications*

EXPOSURE TO THE ELEMENTS

Kaliakra is an exposed spot, subject to extremes of temperature not felt in the Black Sea coast resorts, and walking around it in inappropriate clothing can be a miserable experience. In the summer, there is little shade offering respite from the sun, and sunhats, water and suntan lotion are all advisable. The nature reserve is closed in winter proper, but at the tail end of the season it can already feel a little chilly there, with no protection from the sea winds. Even if it doesn't seem a cold day when you set out, it's worth taking an extra jumper or coat to be sure.

Walking

Kaliakra Nature Reserve is all about getting back to nature, and the main thing to do is walk. Several brief diversions lead off from the main path, often to a cliff-top ledge offering a stunning view of the surrounding sea and cliffs.

TAKING A BREAK

Cape Kaliakra Restaurant ££ If all that sea air and exploring gets you a bit out of breath, the main path eventually brings you to a small restaurant, where you can enjoy a pick-me-up overlooking the waves.
ⓐ At the museum entrance (see page 69)

Dobrich

A charming town that has truly embraced the café culture of the Mediterranean, Dobrich is a good stop-off point if you're travelling between the coast and the Romanian border, but it merits a visit anyway. Not as overwhelmed by the tourism and property fever that have galvanised the coastal towns, Dobrich's citizens just go nonchalantly about their business, which seems mostly to be relaxing, eating and drinking. Its main square is peopled with carefree individuals who seem to belie their country's difficult recent history. The vibe is almost studenty: happy-go-lucky and laissez-faire.

Here, tourist kitsch is avoided; the bars, restaurants and clubs do a fine line in casual chic and could hold their own alongside the establishments of Bulgaria's larger resorts and towns. Whether you want to sip a cappuccino while watching the world go by, pose over cocktails with the town's trendy set or dance until daylight, Dobrich has something to suit your leisure needs.

One of the best places to take it easy is the town park, a beautifully landscaped area that is far bigger than you would expect to find in a relatively small town. With climbing frames for the children and cafés for the adults, it's the perfect place for the family to visit.

❷ The most important of the roads serving Bulgaria's coast pass through Dobrich, which lies 37 km (23 miles) from the Romanian border. From the town, it's a straight drive to the border towns of Kardam and Silistra, and you can also reach Varna and the northern resorts, which makes the town an ideal stopping-off point if you're continuing your journey by car. Trains and buses also serve Dobrich.

THINGS TO SEE & DO

Etnografski Muzei (Ethnographical Museum)
Full of farming equipment and traditional costumes, Dobrich's Ethnographical Museum is one of the more engaging of its kind.

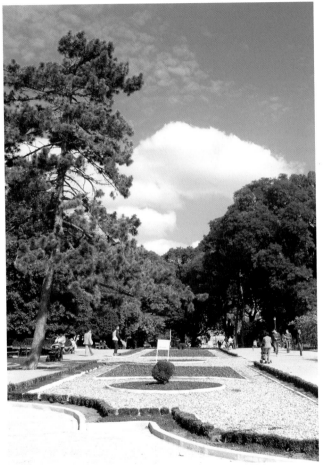

⬤ *Soak up the sunshine in Dobrich's town park*

Unfortunately, the opening hours can be a bit erratic, so you may have to just knock at the door and hope somebody answers. The converted black-and-white 19th-century house is striking in itself.

ⓐ ul 25 Septemvri ⓛ 09.00–17.00 Mon–Fri but closed for lunch; closed Sat & Sun ⓘ Admission charge

Izkustvo Galerija (Art Gallery)

A well-organised collection of paintings, sculpture, graphics and plastic arts, mostly contemporary, but with the odd piece dating back further. The majority of artists whose work is on show are Bulgarian, but there are a few pieces by other Europeans. The gallery hosts occasional opening events and themed collections, mainly grouped by nationality or region. Children's art and photography are two typical examples. The informative website provides a comprehensive list of the exhibitors, works and upcoming events.

ⓐ Balgariya 14 ⓣ 0586 02215 ⓦ www.dobrichgallery.org
ⓔ gallerydobrich@hotmail.com ⓛ 09.00–12.30, 13.30–18.00 Mon–Fri, closed Sat & Sun ⓘ Admission charge

Muzei Yordan Yovkov (Yordan Yovkov Museum)

Named after one of Bulgaria's most famous 20th-century writers, the museum houses a selection of old pictures and artefacts, including personal belongings, relating to the life of Yovkov and a couple of his contemporaries. An English-language information sheet is available.

ⓐ ul Gen Gurko 4, intersection of ul 25 Septemvri and Otets Paisii, opposite the park ⓣ 0586 03213 ⓛ 08.00–12.00, 13.00–17.00 Mon–Fri; closed Sat & Sun ⓘ Admission charge

Stariyat Dobrich (Old Dobrich)

Dobrich was once a famous arts and crafts centre, and this period of its history is commemorated in the old quarter, where pottery, jewellery and woodcarvings are among the souvenirs made and sold in various workshops.

ⓐ ul 25 Septemvri 37 ⓛ 08.00–18.00 daily (summer); 08.30–18.00 daily (winter)

TAKING A BREAK

Bars & cafés
Dublin Irish Pub ££ The old Blage Vaize bar has metamorphosed into the Dublin Irish Pub. Good pub food is served up in the usual Irish theme bar atmosphere. ⓐ Corner of Balgariya and ul 25 Septemvri ⓣ 0586 01475 ⓛ 09.00–23.00 daily

AFTER DARK

Club
Bacardi Club ££ Fashionable nightspot catering to the city's chic set, who are entertained by a range of top DJs. Coolly done out with an outside bar and terrace covered by cream canopies, the interior is equally smart. No main meals, but you can munch on sandwiches or desserts while listening to dance hits. It's right next to a children's play area, so if you're going in the daytime the children will be entertained too. ⓐ Opposite the Yordan Yovkov Museum ⓣ 0885 639566 ⓦ www.bacardiclub.org ⓛ 08.00–04.00 daily

Restaurant
Sezoni ££ Smart restaurant of a quality far higher than you would expect in a small Bulgarian town. The surroundings are bright, clean and cheerful, the staff friendly and the food enjoyable. Choose from a range of pizza, pasta, standard meat grills, and cakes and desserts.
ⓐ Balgariya 4 ⓣ 0586 01606 ⓦ www.sezoni.dobrich.com
ⓔ office@sezoni.dobrich.com ⓛ 07.00–23.00 daily

Bourgas

Sea Gardens

Central City Beach

Church
Information
Police Station
Railway Stn
Post Office
Bus Station
Shopping

DEMOKRATSIA
DEMOKRATSIA

PROF. D-R ASSEN ZLATAROV

KNIAZ AL BATENBERG

KALI MARKO

SLAVYANSKA

15 SEPTEMVRI

FILIP KOTETS
OBORISHTE
TSAR SIMEON
EMIL DE LAVELE
ANTIM 1
KNIAZ AL BATENBERG

STEFAN KARADZHA
SOFRONI
MORSKA
SLAVYANSKA
D-R NIDER
GEORGI SHOGOUNOV
KONSTANTIN FOTINOV

NEVROKOP
MOISKA

Arheologiceski Muzei

Iztustvo Galerija

BOULAIR

PISA
PETKO KARAVELOV
OHRID
PETKO KARAVELOV
SAEDINENIE
ALEKO BOGORIDI
MITROPOLIT SIMEON
KAINA KNYAGINYA
ANTIM 1
KONSTANTIN FOTINOV

RAIKO KYUANCHEV
SLAVYANSKA
GEORGI KIRKOV
KONSTANTIN FOTINOV
GEN-MAIOR LERMONTOV
GEN-MAIOR LERMONTOV

VOLA
SV KIRIL I METODY SQUARE
VAZRAZHDANE
VASKOVSKY
GEN SKOBOLEV
VAZRAZHDANE
SHIPKA
Armenski Tsirkva
ALEKSANDROVSKA

BOULAIR
GARDY PLOSHTAD SQUARE

OTETS PAISSII
SVOBODA SQUARE
MILIN KANAK

ALEKO KONSTANTINOV
ADOLFM THIER 15
TRAKIISKA
ANTONOV
Central Railway Station

ALEKSANDROVSKA

APOSTOL KARAMELY
SHEINOVO

MARAGIDIK
VELIKI
SAGLASSIE
SAGLASSIE

TSAR PETAR

ALEKSANDAR
SLIVNITSA
FERDINANDOVA
TSAR ASSEN
SHEINOVO
TSAR KROUM
HAN KROUM
IVAN VAZOV

BOURGASKA KOMOUNA SQUARE
PRAVDA SQUARE
HAN SHISHMAN

SHEINOVO

100 metres
100 yards

Excursions in the south

Bourgas

Wandering around central Bourgas – and wandering is the pace of life here – you'll feel more like you're in a Mediterranean town than a former communist city. The park is the town's centrepiece – it has neat gardens with statues and benches. Cultural and leisure facilities are everywhere, from the museums, theatres, galleries and art shops to the many cafés and restaurants along and around the central pedestrianised area, ul Aleksandrovska. Indeed, judging by the businesses in the city centre, Bourgas citizens seem to have little to do other than sip coffee and tuck into indulgent ice cream and cakes, then walk off all the excess calories with a stroll and a chat with a friend. The town is in fact the fourth biggest in Bulgaria, and the country's largest port, but you would not know this from its calm vibe.

As such, it's a relaxing spot to while away a few hours, and makes an urbane change from the beach-holiday atmosphere of the coastal towns. It also has a sophisticated nightlife ranging from piano bars to trendy clubs. While it is not as cosmopolitan as Varna, it is the central hub of the southern strip of resorts, and if you're heading south you will almost certainly pass through it. Although it might not be on your list of must-sees for the coast, the leisurely atmosphere really has something going for it, and if you stop off for lunch you will probably find yourself wanting to stick around a bit longer and enjoy the social scene. Bourgas is also home to some of the most interesting lakes in the area, which are a magnet to birdwatchers, nature lovers in general and anyone who just enjoys an unspoiled view.

The merits of the area caught the eye of the British property crowd during the boom, and walking around Bourgas it sometimes seems that you're as likely to hear English spoken as Bulgarian.

Ⓝ Bourgas is a main hub on the coastal road. It has its own airport, from where you can take the number 15 bus into town. It will leave you in the centre, close to the train and bus stations. The Bourgas Lakes lie north,

Flanked by a weeping willow, the peaceful Armenian Church in Bourgas

west and south of the town itself. A bus will take you very close to the conservation centre, to the left of the E87 as you go south from Bourgas, although if you want to cover a lot of ground, going by car would be better.

BEACHES

With Bourgas having such a lively centre and social life, sometimes it's easy to forget it's also a coastal town. The beach is within easy reach of the centre, and has some sea gardens running alongside it, home to the city's open-air theatre. It's clean, patrolled by lifeguards in season, access is free, and there tend to be fewer people here than in the resorts. It doesn't have the range of activities of the more tourist-oriented towns, but volleyball and windsurfing are available and there are a smattering of restaurants if you don't want to walk back into town to eat.

THINGS TO SEE & DO

Arheologiceski Muzei (Archaeological Museum)
Statues, coins, jewellery and ceramics plus a popular natural history feature.
ⓐ ul Aleko Bogoridi 21 ⓣ 0568 43541 ⓦ www.burgasmuseums.bg (for all city museums) ⓛ 09.00–18.00 Mon–Fri, 10.00–18.00 Sat, closed Sun

Armenski Tsirkva (Armenian Church)
The small Armenian Church is something a little different from the usual religious buildings in the region. With a weeping willow outside and opposite a small park, it is in a picturesquely quiet location. Inside it's atmospheric, with lights and pictures and a lot more colour than you might be used to seeing in church. ⓐ ul Aleko Bogoridi, near Hotel Bulgaria ⓛ 08.30–18.00 Tues–Sat, 08.30–13.00 Sun; closed Mon

Izkustvo Galerija (Art Gallery)
Housed in a 100-year-old former synagogue, the gallery contains over 2,500 paintings, drawings and sculptures – mostly religious scenes and land- and seascapes from the local area. ⓐ Mitropolit Simeon 24

🕿 0568 42169 🌐 www.bourgas.net/art 🕐 09.00–12.00, 14.00–18.00 Mon–Sat; closed Sun ❶ Admission charge

TAKING A BREAK

Unison Café ££ ❶ Serves salads, snacks, and a range of alcoholic and non-alcoholic cocktails. Desserts and mousses rotate temptingly in a display cabinet. ⓐ ul Aleksandrovska 67 🕿 0568 25252 🕐 08.00–22.00 daily ❶ Cash only

AFTER DARK

Restaurants
Amstel Restaurant ££ ❷ Three-storey restaurant serving Bulgarian and international dishes, mainly meat and fish, plus desserts. A warm atmosphere that's reminiscent of an upmarket northern European pub. ⓐ ul Aleksandrovska 49 🕿 0568 27629 🕐 11.00–23.30 daily ❶ Cash only

Bulgaria ££ ❸ As the name suggests, this place serves up the national cuisine alongside European dishes. The romantic feel of the restaurant is supported by live piano music. ⓐ ul Aleksandrovska 21 🕿 0568 42610 🌐 www.bulgaria-hotel.com ✉ hotelbulgaria@bginfo.net 🕐 07.00–23.00 daily

Maracas Pub and Pizza ££ ❹ A light and airy eatery dotted with plants – the ideal alternative if you've had enough of traditional Bulgarian joints with their dark, wooden interiors. Italian favourites pizza and pasta are on offer, plus BBQ, salads and meat dishes with a range of vegetarian options. ⓐ ul Aleko Bogoridi 19 🕿 0887 879101 🕐 07.00–01.00 daily

Zhelezniat Svetilnik ££ ❺ Traditional Bulgarian hospitality, folk music and food. In summer, they do a BBQ outside. Choose from over 200 wines to accompany your meal. ⓐ ul Konstantin Fotinov 28 🕿 0568 41819 🕐 10.00–24.00 daily ❶ Cash only

◆ *There's a great range of bars and cafés in Bourgas*

Atagen £££ ❻ Chic, modern black-and-white restaurant, ideal for any smart occasion. Fresh and seasonal ingredients served in international dishes. ⓐ bul San Stefano 129 ❶ 0568 12218 ⓔ hotel_atagen@abv.bg ❶ 08.00–23.00 daily

Bars & clubs

Alibi ❼ Dance, Latino and retro all make the billing at this popular nightspot. ⓐ Sea Gardens ❶ 0888 594913 ❶ 23.00–late daily ❶ Admission charge

Bacardi Café-Club ❽ The hangout of Bourgas's fashionable set, this is the place to recline on an impossibly chic chair over cakes and cocktails, and do some Wi-Fi surfing. Two levels play commercial dance music to the in-crowd. ⓐ ul Aleksandrovska 51 ❶ 0568 27629 ❶ 07.00–04.00 daily ❶ Cash only

Fifth Avenue Piano Bar ❾ Dimly lit and very plush venue with live music every night. ⓐ Opposite the Armenian Church ❶ 0889 905555 ❶ 22.00–04.00 daily

Grolsch Beer House ❿ Large British-style pub, also serving a range of national cuisine, in particular fish dishes. Has another outlet at the Sea Gardens. ⓐ ul Raina Knyaginya ❶ 0568 44017 ❶ 10.00–01.00 daily ❶ Cash only

Groovy Bar ⓫ Whether you want Cuban music and salsa dancing, funky 1970s disco, blues, soul or simply a game of pool or darts, this down-to-earth place has got it. ⓐ ul Antim I 10 ❶ 0886 658057 ❶ 10.00–24.00 daily ❶ Cash only

Karaoke Bar ⓬ You might not be quite as talented as the stars whose photos line the wall, such as Jimi Hendrix, but a willingness to have a go is all that's required here. ⓐ ul Kliment Ohridski 2, Second floor, Bourgas Opera ❶ 0568 41637 ❶ 20.00–04.00 daily

◆ *There's a Mediterranean air about the town of Bourgas*

Bourgas Lakes

Bird lovers should not come to the Black Sea coast without taking advantage of the many opportunities to do a little bird spotting. And there are few places richer in species than the Bourgas Lakes, which host 255 out of the country's total of around 400. Several of them, including the Dalmatian pelican and pygmy cormorant, are globally endangered. The site is on the migratory route, the Via Pontica, and it's possible to spot some of the thousands of storks, raptors and pelicans who fly over it each year on their long commute. If you have the good luck and good timing to stop by at peak migration time, the spectacular image of huge flocks of birds taking flight cannot fail to move you. Take your camera and be quick on the button.

Endangered plants, fish and mammals also take refuge here, with much of the 9,500 hectares (23,480 acres) either already, or likely to be, categorised as a protected area. The lakes – Atanasovsko, Bourgas, Mandrensko, Poda and Pomorie – are also a source of sea salt, and mud from them is used in various holistic treatments. The very brave can even take the plunge into the mud at its source. In fact, there are opportunities for swimming throughout the area, provided the weather allows, and you may also go fishing.

While the site is a twitcher's paradise, like Srebarna, it can also be enjoyed by the layman with little interest in spotting rare species. The Bourgas Lakes have a scenic value of their own. The various combinations of reeds, fields and water provide many photo opportunities, and if you manage to catch a sunset or sunrise you will get some classic snaps to take home.

Getting to, and around, the lakes is not easy, and you are required to stick to the permitted pathways. Probably the most enjoyable way to try is by boat trip, which can be arranged by the Poda Information and Visitor Centre Ⓦ www.bspb-poda.de. The centre will also lend you binoculars and has telescopes on the site. The staff will point out whichever birds are within viewing distance Ⓝ Buses stop within 400 m (440 yds) of the Visitor Centre.

⬤ *Bourgas Lakes, a haven for wildlife*

Strandzha (Strandja) National Park

The Strandzha mountain range extends through the European part of Turkey and southern Bulgaria. The national park is the country's largest protected area, making up 1 per cent of the country's territory, and 50 per cent of its flora can be found in the park. It's a varied and beautiful landscape of mountain peaks, valleys, rivers and forest, and part of the park has the distinction of being one of Bulgaria's sunniest places. The rivers that run through the area are said to be so clean and full of fish that you can catch your supper by hand, and the locals see the water as holy, with curative powers. Whether or not you believe them, the fresh air and openness of Strandzha will certainly do your constitution some good. The park's rustic charm, however, has brought it to the attention of developers, and Bulgarian environmentalists are fighting an ongoing battle to prevent hotels springing up and shattering the peace.

But more than its nature and plant life, Strandzha is interesting for the culture that has been preserved there. Its traditional villages are worth a visit both for the charming wooden cottages that seem to have come straight from another century and also for the customs that have survived alongside them. Perhaps the most intriguing of these is fire dancing, when young villagers fast all day before going into a trance and moving quickly over hot embers. It might not please the health and safety inspectors, but thousands of onlookers make the journey to the village of Balgari to witness the annual event (see page 106). There are many other fairs and saints' days celebrated, and it's worth checking ahead to see if you can catch one of the animal festivals.

On top of the cultural possibilities, there is a range of physical activities available, though it is safe to say you won't be disturbed by the shrieks of extreme sports practitioners. The pursuits are of a more gentle nature: as well as a spot of fishing, you can also hire a bicycle and explore the area on two wheels, or even go trekking. Birdwatchers also make a point of visiting the park, particularly at the very beginning and tail end of the summer season.

⬥ *The forests of Strandzha*

ⓐ Strandzha National Park Administration, Malko Tarnovo
ⓣ 0299 72646 ⓦ www.discoverstrandja.com
ⓔ info@discoverstrandja.com ⓝ If you're intending to stay a while or want to find out more details, head for the Strandja National Park Administration at Malko Tarnovo, just a few kilometres from the Turkish border. If you're coming via the coast road, turn off at Tsarevo. You can also reach the town from Bourgas via car or the infrequent bus service, but be warned that the road is in poor condition (at least two buses go from Bourgas's central bus station to the main villages in the Strandzha National Park every day).

> **TIP**
> Take your passport. Strandzha National Park is deep in southern Bulgaria and, even though you don't get particularly close to the Turkish border, the area is considered a border zone, and you may well be stopped at one of the various checkpoints and asked for your papers.

ⓓ *Life revolves around the sea on the Black Sea coast*

LIFESTYLE
The Bulgarian way

Food & drink

Bulgarian cuisine tends to be dominated by meat. Grilled pork, chicken and beef are the staples that can be found on most menus. A standard meal in an average restaurant would consist of meat served with potatoes in some form and a portion or two of vegetables.

In this part of the world, many people still find the idea of anyone voluntarily going without meat a strange one. This is despite the fact that the country's varied geography and temperate climate result in a superb selection of vegetables, grown traditionally in the countryside. Much of this produce is organic – not that the Bulgarians would use that word to describe it. Here, it's just how food comes. Cabbage, peppers, aubergines, garlic and onions are among the most common vegetables. Typical accompaniments are soups before the main course and salads with it, and you will almost always be brought bread as well.

Yoghurt with everything is another theme. Sometimes it seems that there is virtually no dish that yoghurt cannot accompany, and many Bulgarians eat it every day of their lives. You will almost certainly have the opportunity to try the plain kind, usually made from cow's milk, during your stay.

The food reflects the country's politics and history. You'll be able to spot Turkish, Greek and Middle Eastern influences. But the cuisine has also been shaped by the West. Many meals do not differ significantly from standard European or international fare, and pizza, pasta and even sushi have infiltrated the restaurants, especially in the larger towns and resorts that see the greatest numbers of foreign tourists and residents.

This is particularly true on the Black Sea coast. Natural entrepreneurs, the Bulgarians have responded to the tastes of their visitors, and it's impossible to walk for more than a few minutes in some resorts without seeing the offer of a full English breakfast chalked on to a blackboard. Jacket potatoes, Sunday roasts, steak specials, omelettes – all are standard in the tourist areas, which means that if you're travelling with your family you're unlikely to have to worry about what the children are going to eat. Another popular branch of cuisine is Bulgarian recipes, but cooked in a Western way to make them more palatable to foreign taste buds. This usually means less stodgily.

Some restaurants, particularly in Varna, which is increasingly catering to a business and investor crowd as well as locals and tourists, have gone a step further and put together a truly first-class international dining experience. For the cost of a mediocre meal in your home country, here you can experience the highest standards in food and service, and it's worth spending the money on at least one such evening out during your stay.

But the Black Sea coast's main cuisine highlight is the fish. Many restaurants are on or right next to the beach, and the comprehensive list of delicacies will be served as fresh as it's possible to get. Some places even have tanks of live catch on the premises, ready and waiting for your selection. Bluefish, sea bass, calamari, salmon, swordfish, wolf fish, dorade, shrimps, herring, crab, shark, scad, crayfish, octopus, mussels – if it swims in the Black Sea, you can usually dine on it in one of the coastal restaurants.

No discussion of Bulgarian cuisine would be complete without reference to wine. The climate and geography, plus a long tradition of winemaking, have earned the local wine a high reputation abroad. The country is revered in particular for its reds, which are fantastic value and of very high quality. On the Black Sea coast, however, the long, mild winters provide favourable conditions for white wine production, and over half of the country's whites come from this area. Merlot, Cabernet Sauvignon, Sauvignon Blanc and Chardonnay are among the many grape varieties on offer at bargain prices. The big cities have specialist wine shops if you want to take home something really exceptional, but you won't have to dig too deeply in your pocket to buy a quality bottle. In restaurants, it is almost always possible to order by the glass.

Spirits too have something of a tradition in Bulgaria. *Mastika*, an anise-flavoured liqueur of 45 per cent alcohol, and *rakia*, a 40 per cent proof brandy commonly made from plums, apricots or grapes, are often available on restaurant menus. But be warned – they are not for the

A colourful pub in Varna

faint-hearted. As for soft drinks, the usual range of fizzy stuff is available, as are juices, though it's worth checking before you order whether they are fresh or from a bottle or carton if you have a preference. While the tap water is safe to drink, the low price of the bottled variety means that few people choose that option.

On the Black Sea coast, you will seldom find restaurants that limit themselves to offering evening entrées, and while cafés that only serve coffee and snacks are slightly more common, it is not the rule. The majority of eateries are a combination of café, restaurant and sometimes bar. They open early in the morning to serve coffee and breakfast, typically including English fry-ups and omelettes; in the afternoon they might offer sandwiches and salad. They will also present a range of main meals, such as pizza, meat and fish dishes, which are mainly taken in the evening, when they serve until 23.00 or so, although it can be later in the larger resorts. This results in large menus that are available all day, so it should rarely be a problem to find what you want to eat, when and where you want it.

Credit card acceptance is becoming more common, but it is not yet a given, so it's a good idea to take cash with you just in case. Service is usually friendly and professional, and in all but the smallest, local establishments, your waiter or waitress will speak at least some English. Until a few years ago, tipping was unheard of, but now it is appropriate to leave around 10 per cent, slightly more if the meal or service was exceptional. Provided you do a bit of research, you should find many great places to eat, leaving you with plenty of change – and many holidaymakers have extremely happy memories of meals on the Black Sea coast.

Menu decoder

Menus will almost always have an English, and sometimes German, translation, but if you intend to spend any amount of time in Bulgaria, it can be worth making the effort to learn some of the basic food terminology. Listed below (in Roman script) are some of the traditional dishes that you might come across.

Banitsa Traditional oven-baked pastry with cheese, eggs or vegetables. On special occasions lucky charms are put in them.

Bob Bean soup with herbs, tomatoes and onion.

Cheverme Chunks of lamb, spiced and stuffed, and roasted on a spit.

Chushki byurek Peppers stuffed with egg, cheese and herbs and fried in breadcrumbs.

Gyuvetch The name is a type of pot, in which is served a vegetable and meat dish.

Kashkaval pane Cheese fried in breadcrumbs.

Kavarma A stew made up of spicy pieces of beef, pork or chicken with leeks or onions and red pepper. It can also be served on a skewer.

Kebapcheta Spicy home-made pork or veal sausages cooked on the grill.

Kufteta Spicy meatballs or hamburgers mixed with breadcrumbs.

Meshana skara Mixed grill.

Panagyurishte eggs Poached eggs and yoghurt.

Plakiya Slow-cooked fish stew.

Pulneni chushkis meso Oven-baked peppers stuffed with pork or beef, rice and vegetables.

Riba plakiya Carp covered in lemon and sautéed in garlic, oil, tomato paste and herbs.

Ribnik Fish pie, usually carp, with rice.

Sarmi Minced meat with rice, onion and seasoning wrapped in cabbage leaves or similar.

Shashlik A type of kebab with skewered meat and vegetables, which can include onions, mushrooms and peppers.

Shopska salad Tomatoes, cucumbers, peppers, onions, cheese and parsley.

Sirene po shopski Feta cheese with chopped tomatoes, egg, peppers and herbs cooked in a pot.

Snazhanka salad Yoghurt, cucumber, pickles, garlic and walnuts with seasoning.

Supa topcheta Meatball soup with rice and a range of vegetables and herbs.

Tarator Cold soup containing yoghurt, cucumber, garlic and nuts, and seasoned with herbs; traditionally eaten in the summer.

Below are some more general words and expressions:

Bira Beer
Chai Tea
Desert Dessert
Hliab Bread
Izvinite, kada e toaletnata? Excuse me, where is the toilet?
Kafe Coffee
Kartof Potato
Meso Meat
Na Zdrave! Cheers!
Napitka Drink
Obiad Lunch
Otset Vinegar
Parjeni kartofi Chips
Parjola Steak
Pileshko Poultry
Piper Pepper
Plod Fruit
Rezervacia Reservation
Riba Fish
Salata Salad

Sandvich Sandwich
Sladoled Ice cream
Smetkata, molia!/Ako obichate, mojeli smetkata? The bill, please!/Can I have the bill, please?
Sok Juice
Sol Salt
Svinsko Pork
Teleshko Beef
Toaletni Toilet
Vecheria Dinner
Vegetarianets (male) Vegetarian
Vegetarianka (female) Vegetarian
Vino Wine
Voda Water
Zahar Sugar
Zakuska Breakfast
Zelenchuk Vegetable

Shopping

Bulgarians are natural and enthusiastic shoppers, and visitors will find no shortage of their preferred merchandise, be it locally hand-made souvenirs or designer fashion. A plethora of clothes and cosmetics stores reflects Bulgarian women's attention to their appearance, and some visitors advise travelling to the area with an empty suitcase that can be filled up with bargains before the return journey. Bulgaria's European integration has pushed prices up though, and the absolute steals of a few years ago are less widespread these days. However, the cost of many items is still lower than in Western countries and, provided you avoid the boutiques that sell top-of-the-range imported designer gear, a shopping spree will not deplete your holiday funds too drastically. While the smaller villages have a more limited range of shops and stalls, finding the goods you are after should be no problem in the larger resorts.

WHERE TO SHOP

Varna is the undoubted shopping capital of the Black Sea coast – with its unashamed love of consumerism it is hard to imagine that the city was under the communist regime as recently as 1989. The majority of high-end shops are concentrated in the pedestrianised area around pl Nezavisimost, bul Knyaz Boris I and ul Preslav, where the stores rival anything Sofia has on offer. Familiar high-street names such as Benetton and Mango sit alongside designer boutiques. Bulgarians seem to be particularly into accessorising, with shoe shops, jewellers, leather goods stores and underwear outlets all ubiquitous.

DESIGNER GOODS

At the high end of the market, while there are bargains to be found, prices tend to be comparable to those in Western stores, and you are unlikely to make much of a saving if you buy official designer goods in Bulgaria rather than at home. If you do spot big-name labels at dramatically reduced prices, you are probably looking at a well-made copy. You'll find upmarket clothes and cosmetics stores anywhere that sees a large number of tourists. Prices tend to be higher outside the main resorts, so the better deals on the Black Sea coast are likely to be in Varna. For prices, this rule holds in general: if something is imported, as most genuine designer goods are, expect to pay the same as you would elsewhere.

MARKETS

While the upper end of the market may not offer significant reductions, there are plenty of locally made bargains to be had elsewhere, such as in the many markets to be found both in major cities and in the smaller villages. The joy of such places is not only the low-cost items you can pick up, but also seeing your goods made on the spot, often by old women using techniques and materials that have been passed down over generations. One of the best places for this is right outside Varna's Cathedral of the Assumption, where the cheerful women chatting and knitting outside create a relaxed atmosphere, contrasting with the pomp and formality inside.

The kind of market where your purchase is woven or made before your eyes is just one branch of Bulgarian street trading, however. Also on sale from stalls is a wealth of goods that you might find in markets back home, but for a fraction of the price. Places like Sunny Beach are full of stalls selling sunglasses, leather wallets, clothes and belts. There is often a British flavour to the goods on sale, such as football shirts with Wayne Rooney's name printed on the back, and pink and white tracksuit tops emblazoned with the name of the latest tabloid favourite. If you want a more permanent souvenir of your holiday, there are plenty of tattoo and piercing parlours among the clothes stalls. Seaside wares also form a big part of the goods on offer, from flip-flops, swimsuits and beach towels to lilos and other inflatables, plus equipment for the various watersports on offer.

Fruit and vegetable markets also yield their fair share of bargains, and even the food on sale in local shops and supermarkets will seem good value to the Westerner.

Russian dolls have made it to Bulgaria

HANDICRAFTS

As well as lace and knitted goods, Bulgaria is also known for its ceramics, wood carvings and carpets. There are traces of Soviet influence, but with a new twist, such as the Russian dolls on sale in the flea market over the road from Varna's cathedral, where traditional dolls sit alongside versions of today's political leaders. Bulgaria is a religious country, and Orthodox iconography is also commonly on sale, in particular near the churches popular with tourists. Other types of art also make a good souvenir of your trip. Varna's main art gallery hosts guest exhibitions from which you can purchase works, and you'll also find specialised art shops in the larger resorts.

Another of Bulgaria's fortes is its wine (see page 93). The country's geographical position and Mediterranean climate mean it is a major wine producer and exporter. Bulgaria's red wine has a particularly high reputation, but before you pick up a crate check your home country's customs laws!

HAGGLING

While haggling used to be common throughout the Balkans, Bulgaria's Black Sea coast is becoming increasingly Westernised, and the practice is no longer appropriate at many of the outlets in the area. However, some tourists find that at some of the less formal market stalls it is worth trying to negotiate a discount, particularly for copies of designer goods or if you're buying several items. Use your judgement.

Children

Bulgarians love children and they will be welcome in hotels and restaurants up and down the coast. It might not be the obvious place to go with children, but in fact there is a lot on offer for younger visitors and many advantages to a family beach holiday on the Black Sea coast

⬤ *The Big Wheel in Golden Sands provides plenty of entertainment*

rather than, say, the better-known resorts in Spain, Portugal or Greece. Firstly, the low cost of accommodation and dining out means that you can bring a large family here for far less than it would cost to have a similar holiday further west, meaning more money for entertaining.

And there is plenty of that for children. The main resorts have lots of children's activities on offer and you will rarely drive far along the coast road before passing an aquatic park with a tangle of water chutes and slides. Dodgems, go-karting and mini-golf are to be found in some resorts, and you can hire bikes and scooters. The larger hotels also run various programmes of traditional sports for children, including tennis and football. Then, of course, there are the various watersports on offer. Safety standards have improved dramatically, but of course it is always advisable to book with a reputable company or through your hotel. Children's playgrounds are a common site wherever you go in the area and Golden Sands even has a large Ferris wheel on the beachfront. Varna's Festa Dolphinarium (see page 35) is great entertainment for children.

One of the highlights of beach holidays for children is swimming in the sea. In general, the water in this area does not suffer from strong tides and is usually calm. A flag system sometimes indicates where swimming is safe and a lifeguard is in attendance. Bigger resorts like Sunny Beach also have children's pools.

Unlike in some foreign resorts, food should not be a problem, even for fussy eaters. The national cuisine is not too dissimilar to the standard international dishes that children enjoy, and even in restaurants that cater mainly to locals, you're unlikely to encounter anything too spicy or offputting. In the larger resorts, the menus are typically designed with the British diner in mind. Pizza, pasta, chips, salads and omelettes are ubiquitous and some restaurants even have special children's menus.

Cheap soft toys can usually be picked up in the seaside markets, plus the usual beachfront paraphernalia such as buckets and spades and pool inflatables. All in all, there is enough to keep the children fed and entertained, without having to splash out too much to do so.

Sports & activities

First on the must-do list for visitors to Bulgaria's Black Sea coast is usually watersports. Just as the country's ski resorts have upped their game and now represent a competitive alternative to the slopes of Western Europe, so too have Black Sea coast entrepreneurs put together a package of seaside activities that will tire out even the most zealous adrenalin junkie. Waterskiing, parachuting, paragliding, hang-gliding, surfing, scuba diving, yachting, or hiring paddle boats and rowing boats, are just some of the options. Albena, Sunny Beach and Golden Sands probably have the most comprehensive range, but even the smaller towns usually offer one or two such activities. Some have a diving centre. It's quite easy to find somewhere to take your PADI certificate should you wish.

Bulgaria's lower prices mean that whatever sport you fancy, it's not going to deplete your holiday funds too much to do it. Safety standards are generally very high, but use a reputable firm – your hotel will probably be able to recommend one. Swimming is usually possible as the waters are mainly calm and shallow. The larger resorts also have pools and there are several water parks dotted along the coast. You can also find the usual sports away from the water – tennis, football and mini-golf are fairly common and some places organise sports tournaments.

Birdwatching is another draw. The Bourgas Lakes, Pomorie, Cape Kaliakra and Lake Srebarna are among the best sites for twitchers. If you're planning to come especially for the birdlife, May to June and September to the middle of October are probably your best bet, but there will be something to see whenever you're here (see page 68).

Birds are partly attracted to the coastal area's wide, open spaces, and hikers too will see the allure. There are some great walks to enjoy, particularly at Strandzha National Park and Srebarna. Local tourist and information offices or museums can often suggest routes.

But if all of the above sounds too much like hard work, the coast also has more relaxing pursuits on offer. Some of the mud from the area is used in alternative health treatments, and many resorts have spa centres offering everything from a soothing massage to anti-ageing therapies.

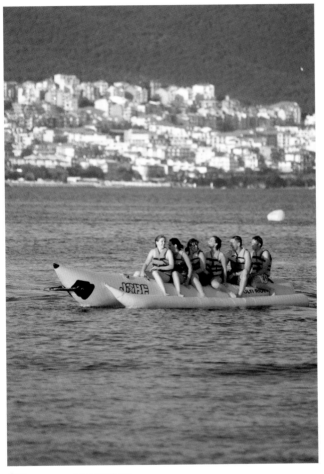

○ Have a go on a banana boat

Festivals & events

EVENTS ON THE BLACK SEA COAST
Discovery
Bulgaria's answer to the Eurovision Song Contest takes place in May.
Cheesy fun as composers and singers from around the world make their
way to Varna to take part in a pop competition. The music is matched by
an array of imaginative costumes and performances.
Ⓦ www.discoveryfest.com Ⓔ festival@discoveryfest.com

Fire dancing at Balgari
The first weekend in June, or around that time, sees a traditional fire-
dancing display in the village of Balgari, in Strandzha National Park.
A religious parade forms part of the ritual, which involves young
participants dressed in white moving quickly over hot embers.

Varna Summer International Music Festival
The oldest music festival in Bulgaria has now been running for over
80 years. Throughout June and July, Bulgarian and foreign performers
stage music, theatre and ballet performances.
Ⓣ 0526 59123 Ⓦ www.varnasummerfest.org
Ⓔ mincheva@varnasummerfest.org

Varna Summer International Jazz Festival
Hosted by the Archaeological Museum, Varna's much-respected jazz
festival runs in August. Participants come from across Europe and
sometimes beyond.
Ⓣ 0523 02322 Ⓦ www.vsjf.com

International Festival of Folk Music in Bourgas
Up and running for over four decades, Bourgas hosts concerts, a scientific
conference, a handicraft expo, plus workshops and film and
photographic activities in late August.
Ⓣ 0568 42948 Ⓔ mff_burgas@abv.bg

Varna International Film Festival

Taking place at the end of August or beginning of September, the festival is open to new films that have not been broadcast in the country or won prizes at other festivals.

ⓔ agrozev@techno-link.com

Apollonia Festival of Arts

Veteran and up-and-coming Bulgarian performers put on concerts, plays, art and photo exhibitions, literary and film events, and workshops and master classes in Sozopol, in early September.

ⓦ www.apollonia.bg

🔺 *Dancers in traditional dress at the Festival of Folk Music*

International Short Film Festival

Open to students and professionals from film and TV, this event in late June attracts competitors from around the world.

☎ 0249 18588 **🌐** www.inthepalace.com **✉** mail@film-fest.org

Orthodox and Muslim festivals

On top of the national holidays there are various religious occasions, including Orthodox Christian saints' days and Islamic festivities. The precise timing varies from year to year based on the lunar calendar.

PUBLIC HOLIDAYS

New Year's Day 1 January

National Day, also known as **Liberation Day** 3 March – celebrates the country's liberation from Ottoman rule in 1878

Easter March/April

Labour Day 1 May

St George's Day, also known as **Day of the Bulgarian Army** 6 May

St Cyril and Methodius Day, or **Day of Culture and Literacy** 24 May – schools are decorated with flowers in honour of the brothers who devised the Cyrillic alphabet

The Unification of Bulgaria 6 September – a celebration of the return of southern Bulgaria from Ottoman control

Independence Day 22 September – honouring the country's independence from the Ottoman Empire, achieved in 1908

Day of the Bulgarian Revival Leaders 1 November

Christmas 24–26 December

New Year's Eve 31 December

◗ Local buses in Varna are comfortable and modern

PRACTICAL INFORMATION
Tips & advice

Accommodation

The price ratings are based on the average price of a double room with bed and breakfast.

£ under L100   ££ L100–L200   £££ over L200

ALBENA

Gorska Feya £ Located 500 m (550 yds) from the beach, this campsite has bungalows and villas (sleeping up to eight) to rent, as well as places to pitch a tent. Though it's not in the centre of the resort, a trolleybus goes to the beach, and there's a shop and restaurant on site. ❷ Behind the bus station ❶ 0579 62961

BALCHIK

Hotel Valeo ££ Bright, bold colours characterise this stylish and friendly hotel, which manages to be both tranquil and close to the town's centre. Rooms have air conditioning, Wi-Fi Internet access and a balcony. ❷ ul Samara 6 ❶ 0579 77029 ❿ www.hotelvaleo.com ❸ hotelvaleo@gmail.com

GOLDEN SANDS

Hotel Admiral £££ Big, brash and just off the beach, this upmarket facility comes with large, well-appointed rooms with balconies, plus some posh suites. Many of the rooms have a sea view. Guests can relax at one of the two restaurants, one of which has a non-smoking area, or in the spa. ❷ Beachside, in the centre of the resort ❶ 0523 90200

NESSEBAR

Nessebar Royal Palace Hotel ££ This classy hotel is close to the sea and many of Nessebar's historical attractions. The 26 rooms include dedicated accommodation for non-smokers and disabled guests, and the place has an intimate feel. There's also a restaurant and garden. ❷ ul Mitropolitska ❶ 0554 46490 ❿ www.nessebarpalace.com ❸ info@nessebarpalace.com

POMORIE

Sunset Resort £££ An enormous complex with separate buildings containing 'aparthotel' accommodation and also some villas. This swanky new five-star resort boasts a bowling and billiards hall, a spa and a plethora of pools. ⓐ Knyaz Boris I ⓣ 0596 36200 ⓦ www.sunsetresort.bg

ST CONSTANTINE AND ELENA

Hotel Panorama £ The furniture might have a hint of the communist era about it, but this budget option is comfortable and pleasant enough. Bathrooms come with bathtubs, and some rooms have their own balconies. There's also a swimming pool and a garden. ⓐ On the main road, near the centre of the resort ⓣ 0523 61025 ⓦ www.panoramahotel.bg

SOZOPOL

Hotel Durna £ Sea views and tasteful décor are two of the things to recommend tiny Hotel Durna, which also has a restaurant. ⓐ ul Kiril i Metodii 56 ⓣ 0888 705023 ⓦ hotel-durna.com ⓔ maria_antoaneta_bg@yahoo.com

SUNNY BEACH

Barceló Royal Beach £££ Plasma TVs and huge double beds are two of the luxury touches at this large chain hotel, a newcomer to the Sunny Beach scene. Rooms are cheerful and stylish, and many have great sea views. ⓐ Centre of the resort, opposite the beach ⓣ 0554 20400 ⓦ www.barcelo.com ⓔ royalbeach@barcelo.com

VARNA

Hotel Capitol ££ Plush rooms done out in sumptuous reds come with all the facilities that you would expect from a four-star hotel, including free Internet access. The restaurant and bar are similarly luxurious and impressive. ⓐ ul Petko Karavelov 40 ⓣ 0526 88000 ⓦ www.capitol.bg ⓔ office@capitol.bg

Preparing to go

GETTING THERE

The widespread purchase of property in Bulgaria – especially by Brits – along with falling air fares post-EU accession, mean that getting there is far easier and cheaper than it used to be. Unless you're visiting the country's coastline as part of a bigger trip around eastern Europe, flying is your best bet. Direct flights from the UK to Bulgaria are available with British Airways, Bulgaria Air and Wizz Air for below £150, sometimes half that with Wizz, although prices do tend to shoot up in high season.

While Varna and Bourgas both have their own airports, both with direct low-cost flights to London Luton with Wizz, Sofia is better served, particularly out of season. From the capital, you can take a bus or train out to the coastal resorts. But with journey times of up to eight hours, some tourists go for the option of an internal flight from Sofia to one of the seaside towns, which can be excellent value.

Another option is to go with a travel operator. Package deals to Bulgaria have increased rapidly in popularity in recent years and most of the main operators offer good-value holidays, which can often work out cheaper than doing it independently, although of course you sacrifice some flexibility. It's worth doing your research before you book. The hotel rating system is not reliable on the Black Sea coast, with even some five-star facilities falling well below expectations, so read reviews from other guests before you commit to a hotel.

Many people are aware that air travel emits CO_2, which contributes to climate change. You may be interested in the possibility of lessening the environmental impact of your flight through the charity Climate Care, which offsets your CO_2 by funding environmental projects around the world. Visit Ⓦ www.jpmorganclimatecare.com

TOURISM AUTHORITY

Further information, including tourist material, is available from the **Bulgarian Embassy** ⓐ 186–188 Queen's Gate, London SW7 5HL

☎ 020 7584 9400 or 9433 🌐 www.bulgarianembassy.org.uk
🕐 09.00–18.00 Mon–Fri; closed Sat & Sun

BEFORE YOU LEAVE

No jabs are required before travelling to Bulgaria, although it's well worth making sure all your standard jabs are up to date. If you are in possession of an EHIC (European Health Insurance Card), the card that replaced the E111, remember to take it with you.

While many people still imagine Bulgaria as a post-communist society that lacks the basic goods and services we take for granted, those days are long gone – you should be able to pick up everything you need while there. However, if you are going to be staying in one of the smaller resorts, or have a particular favourite brand of something, it might be worth bringing a few supplies with you.

ENTRY FORMALITIES

Bulgaria joined the European Union in 2007, which has reduced the red tape considerably. EU citizens can enter Bulgaria with a passport or valid photo ID. Citizens of the USA, Canada, Australia and New Zealand can spend up to 90 days in the country without a visa. South African visitors, on the other hand, do need a visa, for which their passport must have three months' validity when they enter the country, as well as blank pages in it. The application procedure takes up to ten working days.

The bureaucracy has largely been reined in since Bulgaria joined the EU, and no problems should arise from failing to register with the police within 48 hours of arrival. However, some vestiges of red tape remain, so it's a good idea to keep hold of any official-looking documents you might be given. If you're bringing your car into the country, you must carry proof of ownership and the appropriate insurance. You will also have to buy a 'vignette' at the border to allow you to drive on the motorway.

Customs law places some limits on alcohol (one litre of spirits and two of wine), cigarettes (200 or equivalent) and perfume (50 ml). You can bring gifts of up to €175 in value. For a comprehensive list, consult the Bulgarian Embassy website 🌐 www.bulgarianembassy.org.uk

MONEY

The Bulgarian currency is the lev, or leva in the plural, which is subdivided into 100 stotinki. Both notes and coins come mainly in denominations of 50, 20, 10, 5, 2 and 1. Though rare, 100 leva notes are also in circulation. In the main resorts, traveller's cheques are sometimes accepted (although you may find yourself paying a small commission), and you should find an ATM fairly easily. Although the better hotels and restaurants are slowly starting to take credit cards, outside of Varna it is better not to assume they will and to carry cash with you just in case.

While banks close at 16.00, bureaux de change are open for an hour or two later, and in the resorts you will find flexible opening hours and occasionally 24-hour outlets. Make sure you check carefully whether the teller intends to charge you commission, as this is now illegal. Some hotels will also change your money for local currency, but check the rate they offer – while some hotels offer a fair exchange rate, many do not. Changing money on the black market is not advisable as the majority of 'freelance' moneychangers perform sleight-of-hand tricks.

CLIMATE

Bulgaria's Black Sea coast is blessed with something most of us have wished for – a climate that stays mild all year round. Between May and October, the tourist season, the temperature is on average 16°C (60°F) or above. The hottest months are July and August, when average temperatures reach a pleasant, but not sweltering, 23–24°C (74–75°F). The Mediterranean conditions can occasionally be punctuated by winds or a brief spell of heavy rain, but as a rule wet days are few.

BAGGAGE ALLOWANCE

Your baggage allowance will vary depending on the airline you are flying with. British Airways, for example, has a generous allowance included in the fare, whereas Wizz charges for any bags put in the hold. Charter flights also tend to have more restrictive baggage allowances. The best idea is to give your airline a call, or check its website, before you fly to find out what the current restrictions are.

During your stay

AIRPORTS

Having struggled to keep up with increasing traffic, Sofia airport was expanded in 2006. If you fly into the capital, you can pick up the 84 or 288 bus, depending on whether you arrive at Terminal 1 or 2, the latter being more likely if you're flying in from abroad. Buses depart every 15 or 20 minutes or so for the city centre, and run between 05.00 and 23.00. Buy your ticket beforehand. The number 30 minibus also makes the journey. As is the case to some extent throughout the country, if you take a taxi you run the slight risk of being overcharged, although if you find an honest driver the fare will usually be very reasonable, particularly if you are in a group. If you're planning to drive on to the coast, several major car hire companies have an office in the airport arrivals hall. If you need to contact the airport, call ☎ 0293 72211.

From Sofia, you can take a flight to the Black Sea coast. In summer, several flights leave daily. Though private buses and trains go to Varna and some other coastal destinations throughout the day, taking around six and eight hours respectively, the falling cost of flights has made either an unappealing option unless you're particularly carbon-conscious or want to see more of the country from the land.

From Bourgas airport, the number 15 bus goes to Garov Ploshtad, which is also where trains and intercity buses drop off. From there, much of the accommodation is a short walk away. Hire cars are available too.

Varna airport is also served by bus, the 409, which goes on to Golden Sands, and you can also pick up a rental car from one of several outlets at the airport.

COMMUNICATIONS
Phones

Bulgaria has three mobile networks: Globul, Mtel and Vivatel. Coverage is generally good – and constantly improving – and you should have little trouble making and receiving calls and text messages in your resort, although coverage may be patchier in mountain areas. Public telephones

TELEPHONING BULGARIA

To call Bulgaria from overseas, dial the codes listed below followed by the local number, but remember to drop the first 0 from the Bulgarian number.

From the UK 00 359
From the US and Canada 011 359
From Australia and New Zealand 00 11 359
From South Africa 090 359

TELEPHONING ABROAD

To make a call abroad from Bulgaria, dial the codes listed below followed by the local number, again minus the initial 0.

The UK 00 44
The US and Canada 00 1
Australia 00 61
New Zealand 00 64
South Africa 00 27

are fairly plentiful too – you should be able to pick up a phonecard in your hotel, post office or some public buildings. Failing that, post offices often have special rooms where you can go to make a call. As in most countries, calls made from your hotel can be extortionately priced and are best avoided.

Post
Post offices are usually open weekdays, and sometimes Saturdays, from 08.30–17.30. Letters can take a week and a half to reach the UK and Western Europe, and double that to get to the USA. Buy stamps, which are fairly inexpensive, from the post office.

CUSTOMS

In Bulgaria, nodding your head means no and shaking it indicates a yes, which can be very confusing for visitors! However, many Bulgarians are aware of this, and when talking to visitors try to adapt. Waving tends to mean the person wants you to approach them, rather than seeing you off. Wedding rings are also worn vice versa, on the right hand.

If you have the chance to socialise with the local people, be sure to clink your glass with every person and look them in the eye when toasting. Not to make eye contact is considered rude. And if you give a Bulgarian flowers, it should be an odd number – an even number of flowers is traditional at funerals, so it is considered inauspicious to give an even number on a happy occasion.

By law, you are required to carry ID at all times, so it's better to take your passport, or a photocopy of it, with you when you leave the hotel, in the unlikely event that you come into contact with the authorities.

DRESS CODES

Bulgarian society is a little more conservative than most visitors may be used to, but there is nothing like the restrictions on dress that apply in neighbouring Turkey. Some of the more formal hotel restaurants used to expect men to wear long trousers to dinner, but generally the resorts on the coast are now relaxed and fully geared up to suit their visitors' tastes and preferences.

While it used to be illegal, these days you shouldn't encounter any problems if you sunbathe topless, although it is better to find a secluded spot on the beach if possible. Some beaches also have special areas for nude bathing.

ELECTRICITY

The system here requires the common continental European two-pin plugs. You can pick up an adaptor from the airport on your way out. The supply is 220 volts, so UK appliances should work fine.

EMERGENCIES

Should you fall ill and require medical attention, your best bet is to find your nearest health centre. If you are in your hotel, ask at reception for advice and assistance. If the problem is very serious, phone an

EMERGENCY NUMBERS
Medical 150
Fire 160
Police 166
European emergency number 122

EMERGENCY PHRASES
Help!   Помощ!   Pomosht!
Fire!   Пожар!   Pozhar!
Stop!   Стоп!/Спри!   Stop!/Spri!

ambulance or go straight to hospital. Emergency treatment can be sought at: Emergency Medical Centre ⓐ ul Bregalitsa 3, Varna ⓘ 0526 34880; and Bourgas City Hospital ⓐ ul Stefan Stambolou 73 ⓘ 0568 10547

If you need the police, call the emergency number directly or ask your hotel receptionist to do so for you. Should you need the assistance of the embassy, the nearest one is in Sofia, though some countries have a consulate in Varna.

Embassies & consulates
Australia ⓘ 02 946 1334
Canada ⓘ 02 969 9710
South Africa ⓘ 02 939 5015
UK ⓘ 02 933 9222
USA ⓘ 02 937 5100

GETTING AROUND

The best way of getting around depends on your plans. Most resorts, with the possible exception of Sunny Beach, can easily be covered on foot. The main attractions, restaurant and entertainment districts and beaches are typically within walking distance of each other and the town centres often have pedestrianised areas. Sunny Beach is more spread out than the other resorts, but there is a bus service, and in any case the beach and a selection of clubs, restaurants and shops should all be within easy reach of your hotel.

However, if you intend to see several of the towns on the coast, you are better off with your own vehicle. Driving is the most convenient way to see all that Bulgaria's Black Sea coast has to offer, especially as some of the more interesting natural sites are difficult, if not impossible, to reach on public transport.

Car hire

Most major points, including the airports and larger cities, have car hire outlets, and the top international rental firms are represented here. Your hotel should also be able to help you arrange a vehicle. Hiring a car in Bulgaria is more expensive than the general cost of living, and you should expect to pay well over 60 leva per day. Prices can be lower if you book in advance or through your travel agent, or if you go to a local firm rather than a big-name international company. However, expect the quality of the vehicle to reflect the price.

Another option for non-drivers, or anyone who is not confident getting behind the wheel in a foreign country, is to hire a car with a driver. This service is provided by car hire companies, or you could try approaching a taxi driver and negotiating with him directly.

Public transport

The Black Sea coast's more remote highlights tend to be difficult to reach by public transport, but travelling between towns under your own steam is possible with some advance planning. Trains will take you into Varna or Bourgas, but once on the coast there is no rail service and you will have to go by road.

Varna is the main public transport hub on the coast, and dozens of different bus services leave from the town, many of which go up and down the coast to the other resorts. The main stop is in front of the cathedral. For enquiries, call ☎ 0524 48349. Outside Varna, the resorts usually post the bus destinations and departure times on the windows of the bus station ticket office. Private minibuses supplement the official buses.

For a more scenic ride, you can take a boat to Balchik, Sunny Beach, Nessebar or Bourgas, and some boat trips are also available between the other resorts. You will often see the details posted on a sign at the departure point on the beach.

DRIVING RULES & CONDITIONS

Like the rest of mainland Europe, cars drive on the right-hand side of the road. The speed limit for cars is 50 kph (30 mph) inside the towns, 90 kph (55 mph) outside and 130 kph (80 mph) on the highway.

Your driving licence from home will suffice. Wearing a seatbelt is compulsory, and you can only use your mobile phone while driving if you have a hands-free set. If you're spotted infringing either of these laws, or speeding, you are liable for a stiff on-the-spot fine and having your licence suspended for three months.

Road conditions vary considerably. Some of the resorts are small and hilly, and as a result the roads may be narrow and steep, and badly parked cars in the busier towns can make turning, parking and negotiating some bends fairly tricky. On main highways between the larger towns, road surfaces are as you would expect at home and a central reservation is often in place. However, some of the minor roads are of poorer quality, with uneven surfaces and potholes. Also on these lesser-used routes, the road can sometimes narrow to less than two car widths, and you will be obliged to go off road to pass oncoming vehicles.

Street signs too can be confusing. At times absent entirely, at times only in the Cyrillic alphabet, and at times contradictory, they cannot be relied upon – and anyone intending to do a lot of driving is advised to invest in a detailed map of the region and take their cues mainly from that.

Another good idea is to avoid driving at night where possible. In parts, the coast road that runs between the resorts is not lit, and with many bends to contend with, the journey can be fraught. Stick to driving during daylight hours to avoid the worry.

Bear in mind that tourist transport is a magnet for pickpockets, so take the usual precautions.

HEALTH, SAFETY & CRIME

Bulgarian food and drink are unlikely to pose any problems during your stay. The tap water is safe to drink, but most tourists prefer bottled mineral water because it costs so little. While standards of restaurant hygiene are usually exemplary, if you go off the beaten track use your judgement.

Medical treatment is provided free of charge to EU citizens, as long as you can show your passport and your European Health Insurance Card (EHIC). You will have to pay for any medicine, however. The British Embassy website (ⓦ ukinbulgaria.fco.gov.uk) has a short list of English-speaking doctors. Ask your hotel receptionist to help you if you need it.

Tourists are unlikely to encounter any serious trouble. The country has been struggling to get its organised crime under control, but out in the resorts there is little outward evidence of this. Prostitution can be a problem, particularly around certain discos and clubs in the main resorts, and the women sometimes collude with groups of thieves. Prostitutes also sometimes solicit in the clubs themselves. Though they will generally leave couples and families alone, they may hassle lone males or groups of men.

Bulgarian police are fairly easy to spot due to their military-style uniforms. The country has greatly cleaned up its act and is doing its best to tackle its serious levels of corruption. While a few years ago foreign motorists feared being stopped and fined, now the traffic police take little interest in tourists unless they are overtly flouting the traffic laws.

Bulgaria's Black Sea coast feels a safe region for a foreigner to travel in, but do bear in mind that it is a poor country and that there will always be people who see tourists as rich, easy targets. Take all the usual precautions that you would when travelling abroad. Don't advertise your valuables, keep your cash in a safe place, and try not to leave expensive items in your hotel room unless you feel very comfortable with the security level.

MEDIA

The larger resorts are very in tune with their guests' tastes, and British, German and French newspapers – in particular tabloids – are often on sale in the lobbies of the more upmarket hotels and kiosks, usually a couple of days out of date. The typical international news magazines are also on sale in some petrol stations and kiosks.

American films are common on Bulgarian TV channels, sometimes with subtitles and at other times dubbed. Your hotel is likely to have a cable package, which should include CNN and BBC World at the least, plus other standards like the Discovery Channel, Animal Planet, Euronews, Eurosport and MTV.

OPENING HOURS

Banks are usually open from 09.00 to 16.00, Monday to Friday. Museums' opening hours vary, but tend to be from 09.00 to 17.00 or 18.00 in the busier resorts. In smaller towns, museums often close for lunch at around 12.00 or 12.30 and reopen half an hour or an hour later. The smallest museums often keep quite erratic hours, and it can be a case of knocking on the door and hoping for the best. Most display their opening hours on or near the front door, but this is no guarantee that they stick to them. Shops are generally open from 10.00 to 20.00, Monday to Friday, and from 10.00 to 14.00 on Saturday. In the main tourist resorts, though, you may also find some shops stay open later, and also open on Sunday.

RELIGION

Bulgaria is a Christian country, with the vast majority of the people counting themselves as belonging to the Bulgarian Orthodox faith. Icons are common, in both museums and shops, and the country celebrates frequent saints' days. There is also a significant minority of Muslims, around 12 per cent according to the last census. However, while the local people may seem devout in the celebration of their festivals and iconography, Bulgaria is not a place where religious standards are imposed on outsiders. Along the Black Sea coast in particular, foreign tastes are catered for and foreign ways generally respected. Though they may not choose to follow suit, Bulgarians are unlikely to have any problem with tourists who sunbathe topless or have a glass or two too many of the local red wine or spirits!

SMOKING

Despite theoretical restrictions, Bulgaria remains a bastion of tobacco consumption in Europe, and high numbers of local people smoke, including around children. Away from the more upmarket venues, where decent non-smoking sections should be provided, the best way to avoid a smoky meal is to sit outside.

TIME DIFFERENCES

Bulgaria is two hours ahead of the UK and one hour ahead of Western Europe. It is ten hours in front of the West Coast USA and seven ahead of the East Coast. It is nine hours behind New Zealand time, five hours behind West Coast Australia and seven behind East Coast Australia. Clocks change on the last Sundays in March and October.

TIPPING

Tipping was not customary in Bulgaria, but the tourist influx seems to have changed that. Now 10 to 12 per cent is common for waiters and waitresses, and it's normal to leave a small something for the cleaners and doormen in your hotel. Taxi drivers do not usually expect a tip.

TOILETS

Toilets on the Black Sea coast run the gamut from squat toilets – mercifully the exception rather than the rule – to designer conveniences with the end of the loo paper folded neatly into a point. In general, the kind of establishment you are in should give you a clue. Some of the cheaper restaurants charge for the use of their toilet, even if you are a customer, and it's an idea to keep some small change on you in the smaller resorts just in case. You are unlikely to come across anything too bad, but in the more out-of-the-way places, toilets and bathrooms may look a little shabbier than you are used to. When you're on the road, stick to the facilities in the chain petrol stations, which should all be fine.

TRAVELLERS WITH DISABILITIES

Bulgaria is not the easiest country in which to travel if you have a disability. Its infrastructure has been improving rapidly over recent years, and some of the larger, higher-ranked hotels now have reliable lifts and ramps, but this is not the norm and cannot be assumed. You should call and check with the hotel before booking. The Tourism for All site provides some information for people with disabilities planning a holiday. While it does not give specific advice for Bulgaria, it should be able to give you more general advice about planning your trip.

ⓘ 0845 124 9971 Ⓦ www.holidaycare.org.uk
ⓔ info@tourismforall.org.uk

🔺 *Both foreign and local newspapers are available in coastal resorts*

A

accommodation 110–11
Ahtopol 60–62
air travel 112, 115
Albena 18–21
architecture 18
art galleries 101
    Gradska Hudozhestvena
    Galerija (Varna) 35
    Izkustvo Galerija (Balchik) 17
    Izkustvo Galerija (Bourgas)
    81–2
    Izkustvo Galerija (Dobrich) 76
    Izkustvo Galerija (Sozopol) 55

B

Balchik 14–17
Balgari 88, 106
beaches 14–15, 19, 23–4, 29, 39, 41, 45,
    47, 51, 53, 55, 58, 60, 81, 118
bird-watching 51, 65, 66–9, 86, 104
boats 39, 120
Botanic Gardens 15
Bourgas 78–86, 106
Bourgas Lakes 86–7
buses 39, 79, 81, 115, 119

C

casinos 24
Cathedral of the Assumption 35
children 19, 24, 35, 102–3
churches 47, 52, 81
consulates and embassies 118
crime 121
customs and duty 90, 113

D

disabilities, travellers with 124
Dobrich 74–7
dolphinarium 35
dress 117
driving 75, 113, 118–19, 120

E

electricity 117
emergencies 117–18
etiquette 116–17
excursions 19, 64–90

F

festivals 53, 88, 106–8
fire dancing 88, 90, 106
fishing 14–15, 45, 47
food and drink 92–7, 99
    menus 92–3, 95, 96–7, 103
    places to eat 17, 20, 26, 28, 31,
    35–8, 43–4, 47–50, 52, 57, 58, 62,
    66, 73, 77, 82–4, 95
    seafood 93
    spirits 93
    wine 93, 101
    yoghurt 92

G

Golden Sands 22–8
golf 17

H

health 113, 117–18, 121

I

ID 90, 113, 117
insurance 121
Istoricheski Muzei 17

K

Kaliakra Nature Reserve 66–73

L

language 96–7, 119, 120, 128

M

media 122
money 95, 114
mud treatments 51, 104
museums 123

Arheologiceski Muzei (Bourgas) 81
Arheologiceski Muzei (Nessebar) 47
Arheologiceski Muzei (Sozopol) 55
Arheologiceski Muzei (Varna) 33
Etnografski Muzei (Balchik) 16
Etnografski Muzei (Dobrich) 74–6
Etnografski Muzei (Sozopol) 55
Musej na Solta 51–2
Muzei Yordan Yovkov 76
Muzeum Kaliakra 69
Prirodonauchen Muzei (Srebarna) 65, 66

N
nature reserves 64–73
Nessebar 45–50
newspapers and magazines 122
nightlife 17, 20, 28, 37–8, 43–4, 47–50, 52, 57, 58–9, 62, 66, 77, 82–4
nudist beaches 55, 60, 117

O
opening hours 95, 114, 122

P
packing 113, 114
parks 19, 64–6, 75, 79, 88–90
passports 90, 113, 117
phones 115–16
police 121
Pomorie 51–2
Pomorie Lake 51
post 116
Primorsko 58–9
public holidays 108

R
religion 101, 108, 122–3
Russian dolls 101

S
safety 41, 53, 58, 103, 104, 120, 121
St Constantine and Elena 29–31
scuba-diving 25
shopping 98–101
    crafts 35, 76–7, 99–101
    fashion 33, 98–9
    food and drink 99, 101
    haggling 101
    markets 35, 99, 101
smoking 123
Sozopol 53–7, 107
spas and treatments 19, 51, 104
Srebarna 64–6
Strandzha 88–90
Sunny Beach 39–44, 118
swimming 41, 103, 104

T
taxis 115
time differences 123
tipping 95, 123
toilets 123–4
tourist information 112–13, 124
TV 122

V
Varna 32–8, 98, 99, 101, 106, 107, 119
visas 113

W
walking 73, 104, 118
water park 24
watersports 20, 25, 41–2, 47, 58, 103, 104
weather 73, 114

Y
Yovkov, Yordan 76

ACKNOWLEDGEMENTS

The publishers would like to thank the following individuals and organisations for providing their copyright photographs for this book: Fotolia/Ecoview page 67; StockaPhoto/Nikolay Dimitrov page 80; World Pictures pages 5, 8, 10–11, 16, 21, 25, 27, 34, 36, 42, 44, 48, 50, 63, 72, 85, 107, 124; all the rest, Vasile Szakacs.

Project editor: Ed Robinson
Layout: Trevor Double
Proofreaders: Cath Senker & Caroline Hunt

Send your thoughts to
books@thomascook.com

- Found a beach bar, peaceful stretch of sand or must-see sight that we don't feature?

- Like to tip us off about any information that needs a little updating?

- Want to tell us what you love about this handy little guidebook and, more importantly, how we can make it even handier?

Then here's your chance to tell all! Send us ideas, discoveries and recommendations today and then look out for your valuable input in the next edition of this title.

Email to the above address or write to:
pocket guides Series Editor, Thomas Cook Publishing, PO Box 227,
Unit 9, Coningsby Road, Peterborough PE3 8SB, UK.

Useful phrases

English	Bulgarian	Approx pronunciation
BASICS		
Yes	Да	*Dah*
No	Не	*Neh*
Please	Моля	*Mol-ya*
Thank you	Благодаря	*Blah-go-dar-ya*
Hello	Здравейте	*Zdra-vei-teh*
Goodbye	Довиждане	*Do-vizh-dan-eh*
Excuse me	Извинете	*Iz-vin-eh-the*
Sorry	Съжалявам	*Sa-zhal-ya-vam*
That's okay	Няма проблеми	*Nya-ma prob-lem-i*
To	До	*Doh*
From	От	*Ot*
I don't understand	Не разбирам	*Neh raz-bir-am*
Do you speak English?	Говорите ли английски?	*Go-vo-ri-teh li an-glee-ski?*
Good morning	Добро утро	*Do-bro u-tro*
Good afternoon	Добър ден	*Do-bar den*
Good evening	Добър вечер	*Do-bar ve-cher*
Goodnight	Лека нощ	*Lek-ah nosht*
My name is ...	Казвам се	*Kaz-vam se*
NUMBERS		
One	Едно	*Ed-no*
Two	Две	*Dveh*
Three	Три	*Trih*
Four	Четири	*Che-ti-ri*
Five	Пет	*Pet*
Six	Шест	*Shess*
Seven	Седем	*Sed-em*
Eight	Осем	*O-sem*
Nine	Девет	*Dev-et*
Ten	Десет	*Dess-et*
Eleven	Единайсет	*E-di-nai-set*
Twelve	Дванайсет	*Dva-nai-set*
Twenty	Двайсет	*Dvai-set*
Fifty	Петдесет	*Pet*
One hundred	Сто	*Sto*
One thousand	Хиляда	*Hil*
SIGNS & NOTICES		
Airport	Летище/Аерогара	*Le-t*
Railway station	Ж. П. Гара	*Zhe*
Smoking/	Пушенто позволено/	*Pu-s*
Non-smoking	Пушенто забранено	*Pu-s*